VIRGINIA SORENSEN

Virginia Sorensen

VIRGINIA SORENSEN

PIONEERING MORMON AUTHOR

STEPHEN CARTER

SIGNATURE BOOKS | 2023 | SALT LAKE CITY

To Laura Hamblin,
who broke my brain
so I could finally see outside

The opinions expressed in this book are not necessarily those of the publisher.

Design by Jason Francis.

FIRST EDITION | 2023

LIBRARY OF CONGRESS CONTROL NUMBER: 2022949971

Paperback ISBN: 978-1-56085-458-6
Ebook ISBN: 978-1-56085-437-1

CONTENTS

INTRODUCTION

The question you may be asking as you skim this first paragraph is, "Why should I be interested in Virginia Sorensen? I mean, she published mainly during the 1940s, '50s, and '60s. How could anything she wrote possibly have relevance today?"

Even though her novels were indeed published three-plus generations ago, I am convinced that they are more relevant to contemporary Mormons *and* post-Mormons than anything being written today. Open one of Sorensen's LDS novels, and, no matter where you are on the belief spectrum, you'll gasp with recognition. In her gentle, lyrical, insightful prose, your own experience—as humdrum or as dramatic as it may be—will take on a poetry, a nostalgia, a widening that will follow you for the rest of your life.

How do I know? Well, in college I read *A Little Lower than the Angels*, and twenty years later when I was asked whom I would most like to write a brief biography about, the first name that came to mind was Virginia Sorensen. The taste of that novel was still on my tongue, and I wanted to read all her work. I wanted to soak in it. I wanted to be a part of bringing her extraordinary writing into the light one more time.

How could a woman born in 1912, writing about Latter-day Saints in Utah and Denmark, speak so presciently of the peculiar thoughts, emotions, and struggles of Mormons and post-Mormons in the internet age? Much of it has to do with the period she inhabited, which was much like the context today's adults grew up in.

She was born in Provo, Utah, only a year after its first railroad station was completed, and then moved south with her family to Manti,

Utah, and then north to American Fork, Utah, for her high school years. So her childhood was spent in small, tight-knit Mormon communities, where, as she put it, "nothing is long ago."

Similarly, most of today's LDS adults grew up in a tight-knit ward community that functioned a lot like Sorensen's small Mormon towns, where very little of the outside world intruded, providing a seemingly idyllic, sheltered space for childhood to blossom.

But, in the early twentieth century, Utah and Mormonism were on the cusp of significant changes. The railroad, which Virginia's father worked for, had introduced a new connection to the outside world. By the time Virginia went to college, she was able to travel to Missouri to spend a year training in journalism. Then, her marriage to Frederick C. Sorensen launched her on a twenty-five-year tour of America as she followed him from college to college.

Just as Virginia's world suddenly and irrevocably grew from provincial to national, so did the world of today's average American Mormon. Yes, we had television, cars, airplanes, books, magazines, and newspapers, but our religious world view, from which we derived our identity, was carefully curated by the correlated curriculum the LDS Church had developed during the 1960s. The correct information was identified and fed to us constantly. The boundaries the church put up didn't look like boundaries, they looked like protective walls.

But then the internet came, and we suddenly had access to vast stores of information, both about the world and about Mormonism. The LDS Church's boundaries suddenly looked restrictive, perhaps even deceitful, and now they were very easy to penetrate. And when we came out the other side, we found out that the Mormon fortress was a tiny part of a world that was much bigger than we had ever thought possible.

Interestingly, Sorensen's first novel, *A Little Lower than the Angels*, looks a lot like the beginning of many faith crises (Mormon and other), presenting a much more complex and human version of the official, whitewashed version of Mormon history. But she didn't get her information from the internet. She got it from her own research in Nauvoo, Illinois, much of the novel being written in the Nauvoo House, a hotel whose construction was launched by one of church founder Joseph Smith's 1840s revelations.

So, yes, you could say that Virginia Sorensen went through what we today call a faith crisis, the same kind that has resulted in a mass outmigration from the LDS Church during the first few decades of the 2000s. But Sorensen had one thing that most of today's Mormons don't have, and it set her up to write some of the most extraordinary novels ever produced by the LDS tradition.

And that one thing was having one foot inside and one foot outside the LDS Church. Virginia's mother's mother had left the church some years before Virginia's birth, allowing Virginia's mother the latitude to gravitate toward Christian Science. Meanwhile, Virginia described her father as a "Jack-Mormon," nominally a church member, but not very practicing. However, Virginia was baptized a Mormon and attended church meetings regularly throughout her youth, even going to Brigham Young University and getting married for "time and eternity" in the temple. And her childhood in Manti and best-friendship with the local ward bishop's daughter steeped her in Mormon community and lore.

So when Virginia encountered the complexities of Mormon history—even when she encountered the complexities of the wider world—they did not threaten her world view and identity. She had an apostate grandmother, a Christian Scientist mother, and a Jack-Mormon father, all of whom she loved and admired. She could approach these new complexities less as attacks on her soul and more as a new world to explore. Instead of following the lead of previous Mormon writers who defended Zion at all costs, or non-Mormon writers who worked to warn the world of the so-called Mormon menace, she became an ethnographic novelist of Mormonism, presenting a detailed view of the lives and struggles of her people as only an insider/outsider could.

Then there is Sorensen's obvious love for every character in her books. Each one has a complex soul and unique beauties. The believing Mormon is treated with as much poetry as the former Mormon, orbiting each other in a graceful (if sometimes heartbreaking) dance powered by both their inherent value and deep differences. Mormon readers who encounter Virginia's work from an orthodox perspective will find themselves tenderly portrayed, often coming to understand things about themselves that they had never known before—both the beauty and the complexity of their faith. Meanwhile the post-Mormon reader will be reminded of the beauties of their lost faith but also of the extraordinary world that they discovered beyond it. It will probably surprise both kinds of readers to realize that Virginia is no prude. The physicality of the body is every bit as essential to the workings of her novels as the ethereality of the soul. In fact, they seem to rely upon each other. If God is anything like Virginia Sorensen, we are all going to be just fine at the judgment bar.

But while Virginia Sorensen produced nationally well-received novels about Mormonism, what she is most remembered for today are her many children's novels, especially *Plain Girl*, which won a Child Study Award, and *Miracles on Maple Hill*, which won the 1957 Newbery Award—the highest honor in American children's literature. In fact, these are the only books she authored that are still in print. In other words, her children's books have had a bigger impact on American literature than any of the novels she wrote for adults. Add to this the number of times Virginia said that she most enjoyed writing for children, and we see that these books are indispensable to understanding her both as a writer and as a person.

Sadly, though Sorensen was a popular and respected author in her day, the majority of her books had gone out of print well before her death in 1991. However, she lived to see a few resurgences of interest in her Mormon-themed work: once in 1980 when *Dialogue: A Journal of Mormon Thought* focused part of an issue on her, and in 1989 and 1990 when the Association for Mormon Letters dedicated part of two annual conferences to her work. Then, a few years after her death, in the late 1990s, Signature Books reprinted three of her novels, *A Little Lower than the Angels*, *The Evening and the Morning*, and *Where Nothing is Long Ago*.

I believe it is time to rediscover Virginia Sorensen. She speaks with a unique urgency and clarity to twenty-first-century Mormons and post-Mormons, and, with ebooks, we can now keep her work permanently available so that current and future generations may be nourished by this extraordinary author and her novels.

This brief biography is the result of work far beyond my own. I only gathered together what many people had spent so much time and energy to make available. Probably the first person to thank is

Mary Lythgoe Bradford, one of the early editors of *Dialogue: A Journal of Mormon Thought*, who led the effort to keep Virginia and her work in the public eye. The second is Anna Marie Smith, Virginia's long-time friend and correspondent. The letters Virginia wrote to Anna Marie (and that she kept and donated to the Merrill-Cazier Library at Utah State University in Logan) contain invaluable insight into her writing career and provided much of the outline for this book. The third is Susan Elizabeth Howe, a now-retired professor of English at Brigham Young University, who provided so many elegant articles about Virginia's work and who preserved her "little books" in the L. Tom Perry Special Collections in Brigham Young University's Harold B. Lee Library. BYU librarian/archivist Dennis Rowley, whose efforts brought copies of so many of Virginia's papers from Boston University to BYU—not to mention some exclusive records! And Mary Kenyon who gathered many memories from Virginia during the last months of her life. Let's not forget Gordon Daines, another BYU librarian/archivist, who took pity on this poor independent researcher during the COVID pandemic (I was at the Perry Special Collections on the very day BYU told its students to go home. What an interesting lunch that was!) and helped me to get access to Special Collections. I am also indebted to Janet Woods, whose Hurry Hill Maple Farm Museum in Edinboro, Pennsylvania, includes a permanent exhibit dedicated to *Miracles on Maple Hill*.

And how about those LDS scholars who wrote papers about Virginia over the past half century? People like Bill Mulder, Edward Geary, Linda Sillitoe, Eugene England (who introduced me to Virginia's books), Sylvia B. Lee, L. L. Lee, Jacqueline C. Barnes, Bruce W. Jorgensen, Linda Berlin, Grant T. Smith, Shirley Brockbank Paxman, Newell G. Bringhurst, Helynne H. Hansen, Laurie Illinois Rodriguez, Joshua Rodriguez, LuDene F. Dallimore, and Kelly Thompson. Not to mention the Association for Mormon Letters, which provided the venue for most of those papers. And *Dialogue, Sunstone, Exponent II, Utah Historical Quarterly, Western Humanities Review*, and the other publications that published those papers.

These are just the names of some of the people and organizations who helped to gather information about, analyze, and promote Virginia's life and work. I'm leaving out all the people who helped her produce her books in the first place. But I'll be covering some of them in the pages that follow.

And, of course, I should definitely thank my wife, who made this book possible in so many ways. And thanks to the Smith-Pettit Foundation and Signature Books for giving me the opportunity to write about Virginia.

CHAPTER ONE

HER LIFE BEGINS

Virginia Louise Eggertsen (later Sorensen and then Waugh) was born on February 17, 1912, the third of six children, to Helen El Deva Blackett and Claud Elmott Eggertsen in Provo, Utah.[1]

She had pioneer ancestors on both sides of her family. Her paternal great-grandparents, Johanne Andreasen Thomasen and Simon Peter Eggertsen Sr.,[2] joined the Church of Jesus Christ of Latter-day Saints in Denmark and immigrated to Utah in 1857.[3] The thing Virginia admired most about Simon Peter was that he included books in his handcart when he trekked across the American plains. "There were many important things he could have taken that weighed less and might seem more important in a pioneer society, but he chose books," she said.[4] Her maternal great-grandparents Robert Collingwood Blackett and Eleanor Mitchell joined the LDS Church in England, sailed to the United States, and joined the James G. Willey handcart company. However, because of the couple's poor health and Eleanor's broken foot, they stayed in Winter Quarters, Nebraska, instead of joining the company on its journey to Utah. That company got started late and was caught in winter storms in present-day Wyoming. Many in the company perished, as this couple, already in poor health, might have also.[5]

---

1. Her younger sister, Geraldine Alice Eggertsen, had a difficult time pronouncing Virginia's name and resorted to "Buj," a nickname that stuck for the rest of Virginia's life.

2. After whom she named one of her characters in *Kingdom Come*.

3. The house he built in Provo, Utah, in 1876 is still standing as of 2022 and is listed on the National Register of Historic Places. Its address is 500 West 390 South.

4. Mary Lythgoe Bradford, "'If You're a Writer, You Write!' An Interview with Virginia Sorensen," *Dialogue: A Journal of Mormon Thought* 13, no. 3 (1980): 18.

5. "Robert Collingwood Blackett," Life Sketch, familysearch.org, accessed May 15, 2021.

The children and grandchildren of these two pioneer couples went their various ways, and Virginia's maternal grandmother, Alice Geraldine Alexander, left the Mormon Church, and Virginia's mother, Helen, became a Christian Scientist. Meanwhile, Virginia's father, Claud, was a self-proclaimed "Jack-Mormon"—an inactive member of the LDS Church.

But what about Virginia herself? "My mother once told me that the first sentence of mine she remembers was, 'Tell me a story,'" wrote Virginia, "and that the second, hard upon, was, 'I will tell *you* a story,' which she insists I proceeded to do."[6]

Stories and books were a big part of the Eggertsens' family life. "I remember when I first began to watch the books [my parents] read to us," Virginia remembered, "when the symbols became alive for me, and later when my sisters and brothers and I began to take our turns at reading."[7]

"As child she read with such concentration that she wouldn't hear anything that went on around her," wrote Virginia's friend Anna Marie Smith. "This so concerned her father that he took her to the doctor for a hearing test and was mightily relieved to learn that her hearing was perfect."[8]

When Virginia was eight, the family moved eighty-one miles south to Manti, Utah, where her father had a job with the railroad. And it was in this small, Danish-settled Mormon town where she spent her formative years.

"I lived in a wonderful, old house[9] ... with a barn and corral of its own behind, and chicken coops and sheep-pens and pig-pens besides a vegetable garden and a small orchard and flowers and wide lawns in front. But inside the house was something infinitely more wonderful ... a little house of my own."[10]

That "little house" was a closet beneath the stairs. "It had a tall

---

6. Virginia Sorensen, "Newbery Award Acceptance," *Horn Book Magazine* 33, no. 4 (Aug. 1957): 276.

7. Virginia Sorensen, "The Books Were Waiting," *National Parent-Teacher*, Sep. 1958, 34.

8. Anna Marie Smith, "My Friend, Virginia Sorensen," *Horn Book Magazine* 33, no. 4 (Aug. 1957): 325.

9. The house is still standing as of 2022. Its address is 177 North 200 West, Manti, Utah.

10. Virginia Sorensen, "World in a Closet," *Utah Library Association Newsletter*, Spring 1956, 4.

window, perhaps eight inches wide, which made one miraculous streak of light to read by, providing at the same time a secret view of the yard outside and of the path by which people came and went. There was also a private rainbow, for the top pane was a little fan of vari-colored glass."[11] And in that closet, she read, dreamed, and wrote.

Sometimes she was able to ply her budding storytelling skills. "I had a Bosom Friend. ... She was wonderful at sewing. ... So my friend clothed my naked dolls while I earned her labor with reading and with my own tall tales."[12]

But it was her fifth-grade teacher[13] who first turned Virginia on to her literary talent. "I had from her that indispensable mysterious excitement and belief in literature. ... So you can understand how I felt one momentous day when she paused at my desk and said, 'I liked your poem.' She told the whole class she wouldn't wonder but what I might grow up to be a writer."[14] When she was thirteen, Virginia was learning to play the violin. At the bottom of one page in her diary she drew two stick figures, one playing a violin and one writing at a desk. "Which?" read her caption.[15] When a friend "sent one of her poems to a magazine that actually printed it, her fate had been decided."[16] As Virginia wrote in her diary, "A great milestone in my literary career (if I have one). My first poem was printed in the Juvenile Instructor.[17] It was my poem 'Leaving It All.' I'm all upset, I'm so happy."[18]

11. Virginia Sorensen, "World in a Closet," 4.

12. Virginia Sorensen, "Newbery Award Acceptance," 277. The "Bosom Friend" was Carol Reid Holt, a daughter of the local Mormon ward bishop. "Our friendship is as straight, as true and as enduring as the pine and as sweet and as lovely and as perfect as the primrose," Virginia wrote in a September 2, 1925, diary entry. See Virginia Sorensen, Diary No. I., Virginia Sorensen Papers, MSS 1686, box 9, fd. 2, L. Tom Perry Special Collections, Harold B. Lee Library, Brigham Young University.

13. The teacher once brought a copy of Victor Hugo's Les Miserables to class and "and gave us the story of the doll, uncut and undigested. Before the year was out I read the whole book from the library, even the parts that I couldn't comprehend in the least." See Virginia Sorensen, "On Teaching English," an address delivered at the Fifth Annual Language Arts Institute of the Utah Council of Teachers of English, Brigham Young University, June 15, 1957, Virginia Sorensen Papers, MSS 1686, box 7, fd. 15.

14. Sorensen, "On Teaching English."

15. Virginia Sorensen, Diary No. I., Aug. 23, 1925, Virginia Sorensen Papers, MSS 1686, box 9, fd. 2.

16. "Sorensen, Virginia," Virginia Sorensen Papers, MSS 1686, box 9, fd. 9.

17. A monthly publication of the LDS Church's Deseret Sunday School Union.

18. Sorensen, Diary No. I., Aug. 23, 1925. The poem, describing the excitement of graduating into high school, was published in The Juvenile Instructor 60, no. 7 (July 1925): 396.

Despite the fact that her mother was a Christian Scientist and her father a "Jack-Mormon," Virginia was very active in the LDS Church. She recorded of her first "beehive meeting" (a church group for young women), "We had a good lesson on 'health.' We learned to leave brassieres and high-heels alone."[19] The Sunday previous to that meeting, she had been in charge of supervising a row of little boys. They had been so rowdy, she drew pictures of them with horns in her diary, captioning it, "The row of 'little devils' I had in Sunday School." But, when not surrounded by young hellions, she loved Sunday school. "There is such a perfect spirit prevailing among us that binds us, as one, old and young," she wrote.[20]

Virginia moved 93 miles north to American Fork, Utah, for her high school years, and there she wrote for school publications and graduated as valedictorian.

Virginia then tumbled headlong into college, full of enthusiasm. She had been admitted to Brigham Young University in neighboring Provo, and was writing for the *Y News*, all while sending out reams of poetry submissions.[21] On July 17, 1931, she wrote to her friend Wanda Snow (later Peterson), "The mailman brought three rejection slips yesterday. That's—let's see—413, approx.[22] Jack London got 5000. 4587 to go. And I'm only nineteen! That's what I call a swift ascendancy."[23]

She went through almost as many boys as she did literary rejections.[24] Her early correspondence with Wanda was filled with hilarious

---

19. Sorensen, Diary No. I., Sep. 4, 1925.

20. Sorensen, Diary No. I., Sep. 13, 1925.

21. Virginia Sorensen to Wanda Snow Peterson, June 12, 1931, Virginia Sorensen Letters, MSS 2645, box 2, L. Tom Perry Special Collections. She produced these submissions on a typewriter to which she couldn't give "any name at all, unless it was merely 'Creature.' It has not a fear for God or man. When you rely on it most, it lets you down hardest. It has no sense of responsibility, and no notion of its proper functions or duties. It forgets to space, just after you have written a line you are very proud of, and lets you write five or six more lines on top of that one, until it is obliterated, and you have forgotten the essence of it, and it is gone forever. It is oblivious to profanity."

22. She wrote a verse in honor of a rejection slip. "And after all, has anyone / A faith much higher / / Than he who drew a thousand pictures / Without a single buyer?" Virginia Sorensen Papers MSS 1686, box 7, fd. 6.

23. Sorensen to Peterson, July 14, 1931,

24. As she wrote: "(July was a poetical month for me..) / ((and a lonely one)) / (((except for Ken, / and Jack, and Glenn)))." Virginia Sorensen Papers MSS 1686, box 7, fd. 6.

stories of her romantic entanglements. As she contemplated one new boy, she wrote, "I find myself not trembling on the verge of a new love, timid from the scorching breath of the last, but drowned in it, and enjoying myself. I have written a poem called 'Fickle' which I consider tremendously appropriate. What a momentous discovery, Wanda! One man's kiss is as devastating as another's, as all-sufficing, as complete."[25]

And her tastes ranged widely. "The red-head has taken his shining light out of my life." "That Californian of mine has been up here three times. ... He says I'm the only girl he ever cared for. Isn't that just too clever, just too original, just too *dear*?" Another "stopped his car a few miles from nowhere, and expressed the idea, in no uncertain terms, my dear, that girls were like blarney-stones—created for the special and exclusive purpose of kissing on a grand scale."[26] "Next week-end I have arranged to go to Mirror Lakes [in the nearby Uinta Mountains] with a new one (a returned missionary; I never indulged before!)."[27]

To earn some money for college, she took a job she described thusly: "People in divers places are going to see me push open their front gates, brave their bulldogs, and tap gently on their screen doors. They are going to be swayed between common sense and common salesmanship. It isn't Real-Silk ... or woolies, or anything more monstrous than enlarged photographs." It turned out to be a scam.

Virginia took a secretary job at BYU's physical education department. "But along came an uncle from the east with a proposition that took my breath away. He lives in St. Louis, his wife is lonely, and he needs a secretary like me in his business. Besides, not very far away from his home is the famous University of Missouri with its very famous school of journalism. ... I leave for St. Louis one week from Friday. My pullman is reserved."[28]

As Virginia's train rolled into Columbia, Missouri, she was immediately enamored. "Missouri U. is a wonderful place. ... It makes the dear old Y look like pretty much of nothing at all," she wrote. "The frat party was grand, and I was immediately labeled a sweet,

25. Sorensen to Peterson, July 26, 1931.
26. Sorensen to Peterson, July 14, 1931.
27. Sorensen to Peterson, Aug. 22, 1931.
28. Sorensen to Peterson, Oct. 7, 1931.

old-fashioned girl because I couldn't or didn't care to manipulate a cigarette. And I don't drink—or pet—which is a fairy-tale of the fairiest order."[29] During her year there, she got involved with various men,[30] including a Mormon geology professor.

But, with tongue firmly in cheek, she believed her experiences were exactly what she needed. "I get very thankful for my suffering, sometimes. Would-be poets must suffer, you know. Terribly. ... Byron said to be a poet one must be two things—in love; and miserable. So I indulge in pseudo-dramatics and think of what a wonderful biography I will have. Like Tom Sawyer brooding over his own wept-over body, almost. Only funnier."[31]

A few months after she returned to BYU, on February 27, 1933, she wrote a fateful letter to Wanda. "Did you ever hear of Fred?" she asked, ready to be breathless. "He's a peach of a prom bid, and a distinguished-looking escort, and he can talk, and he likes [Edna St. Vincent] Millay, and he writes ... and he ... well, he's just oke, I guess that's all. I'm not in love, again, but just faintly tipping in that general direction."[32]

But not for long.

On June 16, 1933, Virginia wrote, "It is all over. Everything. And it is all coming. *Everything*. ... I have tumbled, fallen, fairly [catapulted] into the most typical case of loving-a-man that ever happened to a normal natural girl." So tipped was she that she started writing tiny love couplets in her diary. "Whenever I feel very much, My tongue becomes quite lyrical. But I was silent at his touch; It was so vast a miracle!" "We two shall know a thousand births on other days; Our love shall come to be again a thousand ways."[33] And, in the face of true love, the rollicking humor of Virginia's earlier letters suddenly disappeared—replaced with rapture.

Frederick Chester Sorensen (born 1908), a graduate of Stanford, was in Utah teaching high school. The couple soon planned their marriage in the LDS Salt Lake Temple, which put some strain

---

29. Sorensen to Peterson, Oct. 12, 1931.

30. "Men here are older, it seems, before they tie up," she observed. "Funny, isn't it?" See Sorensen to Peterson, Oct. 12, 1931.

31. Sorensen to Peterson, Nov. 12, 1932.

32. Sorensen to Peterson, Feb. 27, 1933.

33. Sorensen to Peterson, June 16, 1933.

on Virginia's relationship with her parents. Her mother being a non-Mormon and her father being inactive in the church, neither qualified to enter the temple. And she had one other concern. "Before she got married ... she admitted to a BYU instructor that she was nervous about the temple ceremony, and did not look forward to wearing temple garments. The instructor assured her that his wife had felt much the same way, and that because it was the symbols or markings that were important, he advised her to do as his wife had done—cut the markings out and sew them on her underwear. This made perfect sense to [Virginia], and so she did as the instructor suggested." After the wedding ceremony, "at the Hotel Utah [in downtown Salt Lake City] as she and Fred were about to go down to the wedding reception, Fred turned to her and said, 'Let us go down,'" a sly reference to a frequent refrain in the LDS endowment ceremony. "I knew then I had married the right man," Virginia remembered.[34] Already, there was a hint of religious unorthodoxy in their relationship.

After their marriage on August 16, 1933, they set off immediately for Chicago, where Fred was finishing school. "There was the honeymoon," Virginia remembered, "twenty-one days of the most delightful, changing, excitable world."[35] After Chicago, they spent a few months back in Provo, and then they were off to Palo Alto, California, where Fred planned to earn his PhD at Stanford. "We plan to have two tiny rooms, and the Virginia who has forever and forever lived in huge houses longs to closet herself with this man she still loves with such alarming desperation."[36]

By then, Virginia was pregnant. "My baby is growing very real. He is worthy of a whole string of verbs, already with his pushing and tugging and rolling, and fluttering and—and—but there are literally hundreds!" And she started wishing she had more housewife skills. "Why ... did I think I would master a pencil and ignore a needle?" she lamented.[37]

And then the little bundle of joy arrived on June 4, 1934. They named her Elizabeth (but always called her Beth). "You never saw such

---

34. Grant T. Smith, "I Remember Virginia," *Sunstone*, Aug. 1992, 2.
35. Sorensen to Peterson, Sep. 19, 1933.
36. Sorensen to Peterson, Feb. 26, 1934.
37. Sorensen to Peterson, Feb. 26, 1934.

a baby!" Virginia gushed. "She is all beauty caught in miniature. And I shall never forget her first cry: it came wavering down from a sky vague and spinning and full of flying stars." Beth's birth caused Virginia to miss her graduation ceremony at BYU (she had earned a degree in journalism), but her mother was on hand to accept the diploma.

Fred received an offer to teach at a high school on a salary $900 more than what he had received in Provo. But just before he signed the contract, Stanford offered him a teaching fellowship and a track on which he could complete his doctorate in two years. "So we are remaining in Palo Alto on a very low salary but with great hopes and plans for a really big future."[38]

It took many months for Virginia to recover from Beth's delivery, so Fred's mother, Emma Baker Sorensen, who had been living in Oakland, took charge of the household. She had a master of arts degree in domestic science from Columbia, which made her "right in everything, and I could tell that she would continue to be right into the future," Virginia remembered.[39]

Virginia took to calling Emma "Mother Sorensen," and her presence was both a blessing and a curse. Having an extra set of (very industrious) hands around the house meant that Virginia had the time to take some courses at Stanford, including poetry workshops from Yvor Winters, where she wrote a play in verse about the legend of Mount Timpanogos in Utah Valley.[40]

Mother Sorensen would live with Virginia's little family for the duration of their time in Palo Alto. She loved to talk about her pioneer ancestry and her experiences giving household management training to poverty-stricken girls. Both of these ongoing narratives soon took hold of Virginia's imagination, and she eventually produced a never-published novel based on Mother Sorensen's experiences. "That first forgotten novel was concocted from stories that she told about her student maidservants. As I recall, I was gathering these

---

38. Sorensen to Peterson, June 17, 1934.

39. Virginia Sorensen, "Autobiography," *Something About the Author Autobiography Series, Volume 15* (Detroit, MI: Gale Research, 1983), quoted in Mary Lythgoe Bradford, foreword to *A Little Lower than the Angels* (Salt Lake City: Signature Books, 1997), v.

40. The play can be found under the title "The Hungry Moon," in the Virginia Sorensen Papers, MSS 1686, box 7, fd. 9.

tales in an effort to promote understanding and sympathy between her and me—two women who couldn't have been more different."[41]

Indeed, Mother Sorensen had a strong personality that could overwhelm Virginia. "Having a specialist in child care and household arts in my house was difficult for me.[42] So I went to the college where Fred was teaching and found a small room to work in and started to write books."[43] Fred would often clash with his mother as well. Particularly memorable was the time Mother Sorensen, an orthodox Mormon, saw Virginia's altered temple garment underwear drying on the clothesline. "Then all hell broke loose," Virginia remembered.[44]

On June 18, 1936, Frederick (called Freddie) Walter Sorensen was born. "Second motherhood is different and yet much the same," Virginia wrote. "One approaches it with less curiosity, more fear, but with a greater happiness, all told, because the delights of a tiny baby are still warm in one's memory."[45]

Meanwhile, Fred finished up his dissertation, "a new interpretation of [Hamlet] if you can fancy such a thing,"[46] and graduated, taking a teaching position at Indiana State Teachers College. Virginia's adventures as a "faculty wife" had begun.

41. "An Evening with Esther Petersen and Virginia Sorensen," *Exponent II* 10, no. 2 (Winter 1984).

42. "I'm sure that the polygamy stories—especially *A Little Lower than the Angels*—came out of really knowing the domestic difficulties of two women in the same house," she wrote later. See "An Evening with Esther Petersen and Virginia Sorensen."

43. "An Evening with Esther Petersen and Virginia Sorensen."

44. Grant T. Smith, "I Remember Virginia," *Sunstone*, Aug. 1992, 2. The practice of removing the marks from the temple garments and sewing them onto to regular underwear was frowned upon.

45. Sorensen to Peterson, Feb. 14, 1937.

46. Sorensen to Peterson, Feb. 14, 1937.

CHAPTER TWO

HER CAREER BEGINS

"I first met Virginia Sorensen at a faculty wives' tea at Indiana State Teacher's College in Terre Haute one fall afternoon, in the late thirties," Anna Marie Smith wrote.[1] "She emerged emphatically ... particularly because of a kind of radiance of youthful personality," reminding Anna Marie of Lucy Gayheart from Willa Cather's novel of the same name: "a slight figure always in motion; dancing or skating, or walking swiftly with intense direction, like a bird flying home. ... Flower gardens have it for the first few hours after sunrise."

Falling into conversation with Virginia, Anna Marie was not surprised to hear that she was working on a novel. It was, after all, a college campus. But Virginia worked diligently at her novel, Mother Sorensen taking care of the children and household chores while Virginia was away. She spent some of her writing time in "an abandoned classroom far up under the eaves of the College's Old Main [building]. Sitting primly straight on a rickety chair before a ramshackle desk, she would beat staccato music on her typewriter against the background of cooing pigeons under the eaves and tremendous quarter-hour booming of the clock in the tower a few yards away." Tacked on the wall above the desk was a note Virginia's

---

1. Smith would become a dear, lifelong friend and correspondent of Virginia. As Virginia wrote to Anna Marie almost fifty years after they met, her "letters have kept me going sometimes when I might have given the whole [writing] business up." Sorensen to Smith, Nov. 1986, Anna Marie Smith Papers, MS 540, fd. 12, Special Collections and Archives Division, Merrill-Cazier Library, Utah State University, Logan. Unless otherwise noted, all correspondence between Virginia and Anna Marie are from the latter's collection.

young daughter, Beth, had given her, "Dear Mama, I like you and I love you. I wish you rite a good book. Beth."[2]

But a book was not the only thing Virginia was working on. She was also turning out poetry, some of which she would read to the "faculty wives," and, as Virginia put it in a letter to Anna Marie, "the general verdict seemed to be that they enjoyed it so much, because I did. ... I should have liked hearing another reason." Still, she admitted, "an audience is like wine to me." But even when she gave her poetry to more learned readers, she knew that "I probably shall do nothing with these criticisms but write my barren things with more self-consciousness than ever."[3]

The novel she was working on was set during Mormonism's Nauvoo, Illinois, period in the months before Joseph Smith's martyrdom on June 27, 1844, in Carthage Jail. Its main protagonists were the Mercy and Simon Baker family, new converts recently arrived from New York and setting up house just across the Mississippi River from Nauvoo. The family was based on some of Fred's pioneer ancestors.[4] Nauvoo being only a six-hour drive from Terra Haute, Virginia took advantage of its relative closeness to do some research there. She even wrote parts of her novel in the Nauvoo House where Joseph and Hyrum Smith had been temporarily buried after their violent deaths at ages thirty-eight and forty-four, respectively.

"I have studied a good deal this winter," Virginia wrote in February 1940, "the good old library at B.Y.U. having sent me some precious books, but have written only five miserable chapters. I am not proud of them nor of myself. ... I am twenty-eight Saturday. It is unthinkable. In college, I was sure by *this* time ..."[5]

Then, one day, Virginia broke the staid pattern of the faculty wives' literature reading group by reading them a chapter from her own novel. And when Burgess Johnson taught a writers' workshop at

---

2. Anna Marie Smith, "My Friend, Virginia Sorensen," *Horn Book Magazine* 33, no. 4 (Aug. 1957): 320. Many years after writing the book, Virginia recalled of Beth's note, "I still have it, brown and worn and fallen apart. It hung over every desk I ever had until there was nothing left to hang it by." Sorensen to Smith, Apr. 12, 1957.

3. Sorensen to Smith, Feb. 15, 1940.

4. Mother Sorensen's grandmother, Mercy Baker. Virginia used most of the family members' real names for the characters.

5. Sorensen to Smith, Feb. 15, 1940.

the college, she pitched her manuscript to him. The Mormon angle intrigued him, and, after reading a few paragraphs that evening, he told his wife about it. She devoured the manuscript over a week-long holiday and immediately invited Virginia and her children down so she could discuss the story with her.[6]

So Virginia sent the manuscript to Knopf where it was accepted—despite the novel's having no punctuation. As Virginia admitted in "On Teaching English," "When I was writing my first novel I wanted to be very modern and free, perhaps a bit in prose like [e. e.] Cummings in verse. As I dispensed with quite a bit of the punctuation, I told myself that without quotation marks, the words of my characters would blend with their environment. The whole would flow without interruption. I will never forget my first interview with my editor in New York, where I had been brought to do some cutting and rewriting. … He read one page of the manuscript, emphasizing the confusions in the most masterly way you can imagine, so that within an hour back at my hotel I was hot at the task of restoring order to the chaos of 400 pages of manuscript."[7]

A Little Lower than the Angels came out with a gushing introduction by none other than Alfred A. Knopf himself: "I have seldom introduced a new novelist with the confidence I feel in the author of this remarkable book. It marks the debut, I believe, of a major American writer." Eastern publications had plenty of praise for Virginia's debut. As Orville Prescot wrote for the *New York Times*, "Her book is a fine achievement, a historical novel illuminated by an inner grace and constructed with an artistic skill seldom indeed to be found in fiction dealing with America's past."[8] Clifton Fadiman from the *New Yorker* wrote that no Mormon novel "more convincingly explores the minds of the Mormon women confronted with the tragic, comic, and grotesque problems of plural marriage."[9] And Wallace

---

6. Smith, "My Friend, Virginia Sorensen," 321.

7. Virginia Sorensen, "On Teaching English," an address delivered at the Fifth Annual Language Arts Institute of the Utah Council of Teachers of English, Brigham Young University, June 15, 1957, Virginia Sorensen Collection, MSS 1686, box 7, fd. 15, L. Tom Perry Special Collections, Harold B. Lee Library, Brigham Young University, Provo, Utah.

8. Orville Prescott, "Books of the Times," *New York Times*, May 13, 1942.

9. Clifton Fadiman, "Books: Three Novels," *New Yorker*, May 16, 1942, 73.

Stegner claimed that Virginia could "write better than the majority of the novelists now practicing in this country. ... And she betrays constantly ... an acute and original mind. ... She sees through her own eyes, thinks with her own head."[10]

In Utah, however, the reception was mixed. Jarvis A. Thurston at the *Ogden Standard Examiner* kicked off his review with the suspicious question, "Is she Mormon or non-Mormon?" And then he went on to criticize her characterization of Joseph Smith and Eliza R. Snow, one of Smith's plural wives, claiming that she "erred in ... steering a middle road between historical fiction and pure imaginative narrative." But, at the end he finally admitted that "When Mrs. Sorensen is writing about Purrmieuw, the cat, or their dog, or a man's love for a woman—these things she knows and feels—she writes with delicate beauty and candidness. Then she is truly promising. Her history is not."[11]

LDS Church apostle John A. Widtsoe, writing for the church's *Improvement Era* magazine, conceded that Virginia is "gifted in her style and expression." But "the story is not colorful. Only occasionally does it grip the reader. Fire is wanting. As a Mormon novel it is ineffective. ... Joseph Smith and his associates become ... ordinary, rather insipid milk and water figures."[12] But Widtsoe seems especially repulsed by instances of "unlovely realism," such as when "Simon's capable second wife cured one of Mercy's boys of bed-wetting." However, Widtsoe leaves the door open at the end, "She has undoubted literary gifts. Much may be expected from her."[13]

Of the 7,800 copies the novel sold by May 1942, few of them reached Utah. Still, it was an excellent beginning for a literary career. But the attention Virginia received rankled her marriage and relationship with Mother Sorensen. Virginia described the fallout of a fifteen-minute local radio program about her. "Mother had come over

---

10. Wallace Stegner, "Sorensen," *Saturday Review*, May 9, 1942, 11–12.

11. Jarvis A. Thurston, "Utah's Virginia Sorensen Writes Novel of Mormons with Setting in Nauvoo," *Ogden Standard Examiner*, May 17, 1942, Virginia Sorensen Collection, MSS 1686, box 8, fd. 4.

12. Wallace Stegner, on the other hand, said that "Miss Sorensen is too kind: she endows the Prophet with some of her own gifts." See Stegner, "Sorensen," 12.

13. John A. Widtsoe, "A Little Lower than the Angels," *Improvement Era* 45, no. 6 (June 1942): 380.

to stay with the kiddies Saturday, and listened with us. Afterward I was getting dinner and she came out, pale and ragged-featured, and said: 'It's a pity they couldn't have said Dr. Sorensen. Little Professor and big Mrs. Sorensen!' Fred hit the sky, but I caught him coming down, and all went well, in silence. It is so sad, the way she is hurt by these things. Fred must truly do something great before she can abide me."[14] It was a sad turn, as Virginia had acknowledged the essential role Mother Sorensen had played in *A Little Lower than the Angels* when she dedicated it to "Mother S. Who—like one divine— Dispenses Truth and Time."

Meanwhile, Virginia was working on other projects as well. One was a manuscript she variously referred to as "Goosetown," "If I Laugh," and later "The River."[15] It takes place in "slums" which Virginia seems to have based on an old Terra Haute neighborhood near the Wabash River. One friend said the book reminded her of *A Tree Grows in Brooklyn*. "But I'm not such pleasant reading," Virginia admitted.[16] Knopf was interested and encouraged her. One Knopf representative told her in 1943 that "in a year and a half, with my proposed changes, it should go very well. He was shocked over the idea of finding another publisher for it; he said I would never need one." But writer Bernard DeVoto warned her that "I couldn't expect to write about slums, not having grown up in one."[17]

Her other project had been suggested by Mother Sorensen: Virginia and Fred could work together to gather a body of research and then, using the same material, Virginia would write a novel while Fred wrote a biography. During the course of their early marriage, Virginia and Fred had become less and less active in the LDS Church, and Fred was sometimes quite vocal about it. Virginia wrote to Anna Marie in 1943 about how Fred and a friend "sat and talked in loud voices before the [Christmas] service began—all about the 25th of Dec. being a pagan holiday in the first place and the Church taking it over to 'get some of the business'. Ears along the row in

---

14. Sorensen to Smith, Apr. 4, 1943.
15. In the (Boston University) Howard Gotlieb Archival Research Center's finding aid for the Virginia Sorensen Collection, the manuscript is listed as "And If I Laugh."
16. Sorensen to Smith, Sep. 9, 1943.
17. Sorensen to Smith, May 31, 1943.

front of us were pink as pink."[18] So the Mormon rebel Samuel Brannan became "a project suited to our mutual rebellion."[19]

In October 1941, Virginia wrote to Dale L. Morgan, an editor at the University of California's Bancroft Library, about her interest in writing a novel about "that poor Saint and great hero, Samuel Brannan. ... He has always fascinated me—he was such a gigantic success and such a tremendous failure."[20] Brannan was an early Mormon who was called by Brigham Young to lead a party of Latter-day Saints by ship from New York around Cape Horn and to the west coast of the United States, while other Saints crossed the American plains. When he reached California, Brannan became California's first gold-rush millionaire, the first publisher in San Francisco, and "one of the first smooth dealers in California real estate."[21] He unsuccessfully tried to convince Young to bring the Saints to California, became disenchanted with the church, and was excommunicated—eventually dying in penury.

Virginia and Fred spent two years, from 1941 to 1943, travelling throughout California and to Sonora, Mexico, collecting research on Brannan. During some of their travels, they left their two children with Anna Marie and her husband or with Mother Sorensen. Toward the end of this period, Virginia told Anna Marie, "We are both very happy—and crazily in love, as though we had just discovered something fresh and brave in each other."[22]

Then something exciting happened. Wallace Stegner nominated Virginia for a Bread Loaf Fellowship, and Alfred Knopf seconded it. The fellowship covered the cost of Virginia attending the prestigious Bread Loaf Writers' Conference in Middlebury, Vermont. But she and Fred decided that they would both attend, despite the sizable dent it would make in their finances. To prepare, Virginia knuckled

---

18. Sorensen to Smith, Dec. 19, 1943.

19. Newell G. Bringhurst, "Samuel Brannan and Virginia Sorensen: An Aborted Literary Encounter," unpublished manuscript, 3, Newell G. Bringhurst Papers, 1834–2011, box 65, fd. 1, Special Collections, J. Willard Marriott Library, University of Utah, Salt Lake City.

20. Sorensen to Morgan, Oct. 26, 1941, quoted in Newell G. Bringhurst, "Samuel Brannan and Virginia Sorensen," 1.

21. Virginia Sorensen, "Is It True?—The Novelist and His Materials," *Western Humanities Review* 7, no. 4 (Autumn 1953): 286.

22. Sorensen to Smith, Apr. 4, 1943.

down and typed forty pages a day on the Brannan manuscript so she could send it off to Knopf before she left.

By Virginia's account, the conference was a huge success. "The conversation is so marvelous, so spirited, so interesting, that it keeps Fred's inspiration in a state of constant eruption," Virginia wrote. "I've never seen him so happy in my life before. He belongs with these people—and they're so crazy about him it's funny. He is known here as the perfect author's husband, and as one of the women said to me, he overshadows me as often as I overshadow him—both of us do our share of shining together."[23] The couple even got to know the American poet Robert Frost. "Frost seemed to fall in love with Fred—they saw eye-to-eye on what Frost calls 'this God business'." Virginia also met an editor from another publishing house, who, she said, "will take 'If I Laugh' any old time."[24] But Virginia demurred, not wanting to strain her relationship with Knopf.

After the conference, the couple went to Boston, having dinner with Wallace Stegner and Bernard DeVoto, and then on to New York where she found out that "Knopf likes the new book. There's lots to be done—it was such a damn big job—but I know how to do it now." Wilson Follett, her new editor, said "that he is no prophet—but that it's in the cards that I will be a 'very great writer' and that I will 'click high'… So I left New York and the office in a high glow. I'll work like hell, of course—that's the way with such prophecies, they depend so much on what one does with all the energy he has. Thank God I love the work itself."[25]

Back at home, Virginia got "back into the book with a vengeance," retreating to the tower to work through the Brannan manuscript's editing notes.[26] Toward the end of the manuscript,[27] her editor had highlighted a sentence and written, "I will cite this with great joy as an example of how the style tightens and coalesces, and the sentences take on variety and beautifully chiseled shapes, in the places that you specially, deeply feel and care about.'"

---

23. Sorensen to Smith, Aug. 23, 1943.
24. Sorensen to Smith, Sep. 9, 1943.
25. Sorensen to Smith, Sep. 9, 1943.
26. Sorensen to Smith, Nov. 3, 1943.
27. Page 617 to be exact.

"Let that be the dedication for the labor," Virginia wrote to Anna Marie. "You be the witness."[28]

On December 2, 1943, Virginia packed the revised Brannan manuscript into two boxes, and sent it off to Knopf. "I was afraid he [the post worker] would suddenly sniff and say: 'What is that odd smell? Somebody must be shipping a body—' But he didn't. ... He remembered the days two years ago when I got the galleys for the Angels, and he said, smiling, 'You'll soon be coming in for more of those bundles then?' What a miracle! Going out of the office I felt like a veritable giantess."[29]

Even better, Virginia had recently received permission from poet E. E. Cummings to use the title of one of his poems for the title of the Brannan book: "Sam Was a Man."

She planned to clean the Brannan materials out of the tower,[30] store them away in the basement with her notes for *A Little Lower than the Angels*, and, in her newly pristine office, "write the most beautiful book about junk ever written."[31]

About a month later, Virginia received a reply from her editor, Wilson Follett. "I give you the first comment in Follett's book of a letter," Virginia wrote to Anna Marie. "'The first quarter of this novel is written in fire and blood, and the last quarter is written in fire and blood. But the middle half is written in molasses.'"

"At first I wanted to get drunk. ... I stewed in apprehension for a week, fear-unbelief-regret-disgust. I had invested The Angels in Sam and in Goosetown, and what did I have to show for it?" Virginia had been counting on the book sales to cover the expenses that a college professor's job did not. But now she had another round of edits to wade through. The problem with the manuscript, Virginia decided, was that "one cannot write a novel and split it in half with an histor-ical-biography. All I have to do is strip out the sticky history which I felt obliged to use because of the bulging files, and then piece the shredded edges together."[32] Easy enough. But a month later, Virginia

---

28. Sorensen to Smith, Nov. 8, 1943.
29. Sorensen to Smith, Dec. 3, 1943.
30. 850 pages worth, according to Bringhurst, "Samuel Brannan and Virginia So-rensen," 19.
31. Sorensen to Smith, Dec. 3, 1943.
32. Sorensen to Smith, Jan. 5, 1944.

was still struggling. "I have moments of cold fear about it. Follett writes pages and pages. It is essential for my career that I finish the book now and at once and get on to the 'tactically important third novel. ... Some days I work well; other days I don't work at all."[33]

She had two consolations. One was that another 5,000 copies of *A Little Lower than the Angels* had sold, and the royalties covered "the Bread Loaf note and the Semantics Seminar, with seventeen dollars left to pay Freddie's tuition! Praise be!"[34] The other was some fan mail she received about a short story she had published in *Woman's Day* called "To John from Astrid." "They love me because I write sweet love stories without 'sex interest or triangles, which is all fiction is nowadays.' They are going to read my novel as soon as possible. It saddens me to think about when they come to the sex-interest and triangle; they will be disillusioned and go back to believing the world is getting worse and worse."[35]

On February 19, Virginia sent the revised Brannan manuscript off with no fanfare. "I don't say anything final about it—only that it is gone again."[36]

The book came back a month later. "Follett is still unsatisfied," Virginia despaired. "I feel as though I could never touch the book again as long as I live." Follett tried to be supportive, saying, "All I need is a bit of time and rest. Perspective." And Virginia admitted that taking two years off of "If I Laugh" had helped. "I can hardly wait to plunge in all over. It is more important to me than ever. I can't help wondering if Follett is right and that when I return to Sam, fresh and new, the 'incomparable pearls' in it will string themselves together firmly and inevitably?"

Follett was certain that Virginia could find another publisher for the book instantly, "but we beg you not to consider it. In the long run it is best not to publish again until what you publish will advance your dignity and your name."

"In other words," Virginia wrote, "they refuse to publish anything that doesn't come up to the Angels." Knopf was willing to send

---

33. Sorensen to Smith, Jan. 25, 1944.
34. Sorensen to Smith, Jan. 5, 1944.
35. Sorensen to Smith, Jan. 17, 1944.
36. Sorensen to Smith, Feb 21, 1944.

another advance. But "I don't want it; I should be afraid to take it. Aiming at a deadline completely stifles me, let alone worrying over gratuitous advances."[37]

Nevertheless, Knopf started sending her $50 a month "for the purpose of getting help for my household. This happened after a careful investigation of what my trouble was—why I was not writing 'up to my standard'—whatever that is! I hesitated to accept the money because Alfred [Knopf] said firmly that he wanted 'something entirely publishable' by January. And suppose I failed again!"

She was feeling bitter about the time she had spent on the Brannan manuscript. "Letting them persuade me to give up Goosetown for another historical was a terrible mistake that has cost me nearly two years of my creative life."[38] Goosetown had become a "flood inside my skin. ... I am through being afraid because I respect so deeply what I am doing." She had sent the Goosetown manuscript home with Mother Sorensen over Christmas but received more frustration than help from her commentary. She "has written careful criticisms like this all through the book: '... cats desiring at midnight ...' LEAVE OUT DESIRING. ADDS NOTHING. It is a rich commentary on her generation."[39]

Mother Sorensen came to visit for three weeks that May, which was both a curse and a blessing. Virginia and Fred both had to "go dry for a time and behave ourselves"[40] while she was there, but her presence left Virginia free to "run off every day. ... It is wonderful to have the woman come and wash and iron and clean—I am exuberant with energy." And she poured her time into Goosetown. "You would not believe how far along it is—how it is flowing out."[41]

In her excitement, Virginia decided to bring Goosetown to Bread Loaf.

> I have planned the changes in detail, now, and am anxious to get back to it. It will be called The Flood and the river will be [the] central character ... and all through the story symbolic of the rising flood of social

---

37. Sorensen to Smith, Mar. 29, 1944.
38. Sorensen to Smith, May 26 or 27, 1944.
39. Sorensen to Smith, May [no day] 1944.
40. Sorensen to Smith, May [no day] 1944.
41. Sorensen to Smith, May 26 or 27, 1944.

pressures! How do you like that? I write it in my sleep since I actually … *lived* a flood. I have seen the roofs of Goosetown floating and shacks going down in pieces. I have seen the people waiting on the levee while the water rose and rose—climbing their doorsteps.

Godamighty! Just wait![42]

But by June she was laboring over the Brannan book again. "The [manuscript] is now about six inches thick and I'm worrying about cutting—there is about an inch and half to go yet! Too many words for war-time."[43]

Indeed, during the past year, the shadow of World War II had been hanging over the Sorensen family. Fred had been called up in the draft but had received a six-month deferment after a college administrator intervened. But the possibility of Fred being impressed into the military was real. He had been teaching at a Navy school but had gotten into some trouble after he had revealed too many of his irreligious thoughts to his students (largely Catholic) during class. Virginia had told friends that if Fred was shipped off to a camp in the United States, she would pull up stakes and follow him there rather than take over his classes. "If I allow myself to think of it … I am afraid. … The truth is that my love for Fred is such a dependent love—he is the catalytic agent in my life and I am creatively dead even when he is gone a few days. Sometimes I suspect that working here in the tower has been because of my feeling of him so close, where I can reach him if need be in a moment."[44]

And big changes were indeed on the horizon. First, Fred was being courted by the English department at Michigan State College of Agriculture and Applied Science. "He seems thrilled about the whole thing—goes about grinning," Virginia wrote.[45] "If we go, I shall be glad."

But, second, Knopf finally rejected the Brannan manuscript for good. The verdict was: "a good book, but they don't want 'A Steinbeck novel by Virginia Sorensen.' They still speak of 'the dignity of' my career, and say the critics would accuse me of imitating 'Tortilla

---

42. Sorensen to Smith, June 16, 1944.
43. Sorensen to Smith, June 16, 1944.
44. Sorensen to Smith, May 26 or 27, 1944.
45. Sorensen to Smith, Aug. 19, 1944.

Flat,' and I would get exactly nowhere."[46] Neither was Knopf willing to publish Goosetown. With this, the relationship between Virginia and Knopf effectively ended. "I am very sorry things turned out like this," Alfred wrote to her. "I really had great hopes of you."[47]

"So here I am with two books shelved and—funny thing—I hardly feel anything about it," Virginia wrote. "I am simply anxious to get on to something I can truly feel is my own."[48]

---

46. Newell G. Bringhurst has suggested that the book was also "the victim of poor timing. During the 1940s, the very time that Sorensen was working on Sam Brannan, three book-length works on the colorful former Mormon appeared." Two were, coincidentally, a novel and a biography of Brannan by Paul Bailey, the novel titled *The Gay Saint* (1942) and the biography titled *Sam Brannan and the California Mormons* (1943). Reva Scott published another novel, *Samuel Brannan and the Golden Fleece*, in 1944. See Bringhurst, "Samuel Brannan and Virginia Sorensen," 15–16.

47. Sorensen to Smith, June 28, 1945.

48. Sorensen to Smith, Aug. 19, 1944. Fred also finished his half of the project, completing a Brannan biography; but it, too, remains unpublished. Bringhurst, laboring under the misapprehension that Virginia had written the biography as well (it was in her papers, after all, and did not have Fred's name on it), puzzled over the differing attitudes toward Brannan. "In contrast to the ambivalent, and at time positive evaluation of Brannan in her novel, Sorensen presented in her non-fiction biography a generally negative, at times harsh portrait." See Bringhurst, "Samuel Brannan and Virginia Sorensen," 9.

CHAPTER THREE

HER CAREER BEGINS AGAIN

September 1944 found the Sorensen family living in East Lansing, Michigan, where Fred had taken a position teaching semantics at Michigan State College. It was a whole new world for them. Fred was "all grin, all enthusiasm." Virginia was enchanted by the beauty of the campus. "One walks on the campus for hours, finding glorious spots along the river which runs amiably through it, among trees. There are sunken gardens, pools with lilies, wild ducks, groves of trees, and occasionally a lovely building, all by itself." As young Beth observed as they sat in a campus garden, "We could put the whole campus at Indiana State in this one garden."

But as for writing: "Surely I am not a writer now," Virginia mused to Anna Marie, "but all housewife. ... I am lost, wallowing in comfort and beauty, without a soul."[1]

In an attempt to get her writing going again, Virginia went to Chicago to talk with Shirley Collier, a movie agent who had sold the screenplay for *Gone with the Wind*, feeling out the possibilities of "a thirteen-week writing contract in Hollywood." And—how could she help it—Virginia was soon "deeply involved with another novel."

"I'm not sure about the book at all, but why be sure of anything?" she wrote. "I do feel the suffering of creating two versions of The River [Goosetown] has been good for me. ... I have learned a lot that I needed to learn. Whether it profits me or destroys me, I have

---

1. Virginia Sorensen, letter to Anna Marie Smith, Sep. 22, 1944, Anna Marie Smith Papers, MS 540, fd. 12, Special Collections and Archives Division, Merrill-Cazier Library, Utah State University. Unless otherwise, noted, all correspondence between Sorensen and Smith are from Smith's papers.

no notion."[2] She ruminated that perhaps "my mistake with the *River* was the effort to present ugly and coarse materials in enchanting and poetic phrases. I wished contrasts—and reaped confusion."[3]

Six months later, Virginia felt that "our life here has been the most settled and satisfactory of any time in my experience."[4] "It is splendid to see [Fred] happy and busy at something he considers important. I am intellectually convinced that the only really pleasurable success for women is that reflected from a successful husband—but I disdain it, really, of course. A sweet pot to stew in." She was also enjoying Beth (who was now as tall as Virginia) and Freddie. "The children are more delightful every day, and I concentrate on them with a kind of leechy thirst. Sometimes I think I am *too* aware of them and that everything they say and do should not be so significant."[5] But the lack of book royalties, the smallness of a college professor's salary, and the high cost of living in East Lansing was starting to take its toll. "We are broke three weeks out of every month. Rents are fantastic, and everything else remains blandly out of sight."

So, Virginia pursued the Hollywood contract, "feeling that the movies are of our time, as radio is, and one ought to know the inside of them. I feel deeply that where great audience is I wish to be—there are such potentialities for good or bad, in movies."[6]

She also had a new publisher on the hook. "Reynal and Hitchcock are interested in the new book now, and I have at last had a letter with complete understanding in it. ... They are liberal and experimental as well as excellent."[7]

At the same time, Fred was applying for another teaching position, this time at the University of Denver. "It is our dream-city," Virginia wrote, "and has been for many years. The Place To Settle. And eventually our own cabin just above in the mountains—which Fred wants to build himself. I can't keep from dreaming."[8]

Meanwhile, to Virginia's delight, there was competition for her

---

2. Sorensen to Smith, Nov. 29, 1944.
3. Sorensen to Smith, Mar. 8, 1945.
4. Sorensen to Smith, Feb. 27, 1945.
5. Sorensen to Smith, Mar. 19, 1945.
6. Sorensen to Smith, June 28, 1945.
7. Sorensen to Smith, June 28, 1945.
8. Sorensen to Smith, June 28, 1945.

new novel. "I have had the very pleasant experience of having two publishers dickering a bit, offering extra advertising allowance, etc. My ego has been reborn." She was a writer again, but she worried that the book would not stack up to the success of *A Little Lower than the Angels*. "It has come to be almost a symbol of something which I cannot re-accomplish—like a race one won when one was young (what a sentence of sounds!) and cannot do again." The new book, as she told Anna Marie Smith, "has so much of myself in it that if you love me you will like it too."[9]

Reynal and Hitchcock won the bidding war and planned to publish *On This Star* the next year. And, on August 14, 1945, the Sorensen family indeed started their move to Denver where Fred had landed a post as an associate professor.

On This Star was published May 20, 1946, to mixed reviews. Kirkus called it "well worth reading," though "marred by a melodramatic climax."[10] Orville Prescott at the *New York Times* noted "Mrs. Sorensen's true feeling for some of her characters and ... her beautiful prose," but also tagged the ending as melodramatic.[11] Her greatest panning, however, came from fellow Mormon Vardis Fisher.[12] "On the cover it said that she 'studied creative writing' at Stanford. As one who 'taught creative writing' for many years at one university or another—and perceived, at last, that only an ignoramus can imagine or a fraud pretend that writing can be taught—I can sympathize with Mrs. Sorensen in her unfortunate waste of time. I don't know why she allowed her publisher to print such a damning revelation. ... When she forgets what she was 'taught' at Stanford she will write better books than this one."[13] However, "Her feeling for fiction and her skill with words are authentic," Prescott concluded. "This particular book just isn't one of her happier efforts."[14] The general consensus seemed to validate Sorensen's fears, *A Little Lower than the Angels* was a high point she might never reach again.

Dale L. Morgan at *The Saturday Review* vigorously disagreed.

---

9. Sorensen to Smith, July 15, 1945.
10. "On This Star," *Kirkus Reviews*, May 1, 1946, kirkusreviews.com.
11. Orville Prescott, "Books of the Times," *New York Times*, June 5, 1946.
12. Author of *Children of God*, a fictionalized retelling of early Mormon history.
13. Vardis Fisher, "Pantry Nightingale," *New York Times*, June 9, 1946.
14. Prescott, "Books of the Times."

"This second novel is in all ways superior to the first, firmer in its grasp of people, more solidly grounded in reality, more perspicuous and more penetrating. ... In the temple as in the irrigation ditch, her feeling for the Mormon way of life is appreciative, sensitive, and direct." He compared some of her "insights, her arresting turns of phrase, and the rhythms of her prose" to a young D. H. Lawrence.[15]

Edward A. Geary, a professor of English at BYU, initially "rated *On This Star* as the least satisfying of her Mormon regional novels." However, "in the years that followed," he "found it ... to be the Sorensen novel that stays with me the most insistently, whose human situations and local color remain most vividly in my memory."[16] *On This Star* does have a remarkable ethos. Indeed, it is the only one of Virginia's novels that was ever made into a movie.[17]

Around this time, Virginia's old Sam Brannan book entered her life again, but in an entirely new way. She had spent some time researching Brannan's years in Sonora, Mexico, where he had tried to develop some land he had been given. While Virginia was there, she became acquainted with the Yaqui, an indigenous people. Her interest in them outlasted her interest in Sam Brannan, and she wanted to go back to live with them for a time, which she did in the spring of 1947.

"The very night I arrived in Guaymas, Sonora, Mexico, a symbolic incident occurred which I will always remember," she wrote. "It happened that just before I left my home in Denver, there was a shower of meteors. ... My husband and children and I lay on the grass in front of our house and watched them fall." Some friends had warned Virginia that "Mexican drivers of taxis were dangerous

---

15. Dale L. Morgan, "Craftsman vs. Artist," *Saturday Review*, May 25, 1946, 14. Morgan, however, also chafed at the novel's ending.

16. Edward A. Geary, "Joseph and His Brothers: Rivalry in Virginia Sorensen's *On This Star*," paper delivered at the annual meeting of the Association for Mormon Letters, January 28, 1989, Weber State University.

17. Namely, *A Loss of Innocence* (1996) also known as *The End of Eden*, a television movie directed by Graeme Clifford and broadcast on ABC. It was filmed largely in Heber Valley, Utah. The *Deseret News* did not like it much at all, its critic writing that the movie was "as foolish as it is predictable" (Sep. 28, 1996). It starred Jennie Garth, famous for playing Kelly Taylor in *Beverly Hills, 90210*. The screenwriter, Joyce Eliason, was born in Manti, Utah, on which the town in *On This Star* is based. Eliason went on to co-produce David Lynch's *Mulholland Drive*.

brigands with bristling mustaches, practiced in various methods of robbery. Naturally I didn't take this rather romantic warning much to heart—until I actually found myself moving through the darkest dark I ever remember, lone passenger in a rickety taxicab." Her fright mounted as the cab plunged farther and farther into the night until the driver "turned his head and asked me a question which I will never forget. ... 'Tell me, Senorita, where you came from, *did the stars rain?*' ... I have never again been really afraid of any stranger."[18]

As Virginia interacted with the Yaqui, "I found a much more important commonness beneath the uncommonness. ... Even their history, when I studied it carefully afterward, had its similarity to our own. ... Joseph Smith, or Robert E. Lee, or the great Yaqui hero, Cajeme—how different and yet how much alike they are! ... I remember my first shock at the echo in the words and the idea when a Yaqui said to me, proudly, 'We are a peculiar people.'"[19]

"Asking questions of these strangers taught me what questions to ask myself," Virginia wrote, "what questions to ask of *life*."[20] Of her stay there, she wrote to one friend, "I felt *complete*. I wanted to stay in Potam forever."[21] From her time with the Yaqui, Virginia produced a short story, "The Talking Stick," which received an O. Henry Award.[22]

Despite her trip to Mexico, Virginia had quickly produced a new novel, one that took place in the mountains of Colorado and had little to do with Mormons. Titled *The Neighbors*, Reynal and Hitchcock released it only fifteen months after *On This Star*, meaning that Virginia had lived in Colorado only two years before the book's publication. Some of the reviews were worse than those that accompanied her previous effort. "It might have been a fine and important novel," said Kirkus. "As it stands, it is badly in need of blue pencilling, drastic editing to control the wandering from the thread

---

18. Virginia Sorensen, "Is It True?—The Novelist and His Materials," *Western Humanities Review* 7, no. 4 (Autumn 1953): 286–87.

19. Sorensen, "Is It True?" 287–88. "Peculiar people" is a phrase from Deuteronomy 14:2 and 1 Peter 2:9 in the King James Version of the Holy Bible that Mormons often use to refer to themselves.

20. Sorensen, "Is It True?" 288.

21. Jacqueline C. Barnes, "Sacrifice to the Proper Gods," *Association for Mormon Letters Annual, 1994* (Salt Lake City: n.p.), 1:78.

22. Virginia Sorensen, "The Talking Stick," *New Mexico Quarterly Review* 17, no. 4 (Winter 1947): 432–46.

of narrative. Both in style and content, it too often flags and lags."[23] Andrea Parke at the *New York Times* called *The Neighbors* "an absorbing, colorful tale of the bitterness and conflict existing between two families of sheep ranchers in the Colorado mountains." But also noted that the ending was "a pat, happy conclusion too quickly achieved. More than that, it seems forced."[24]

"Same old criticism of my violence," Virginia sighed, referring to the death that triggers the story's ending. "Perhaps I am wrong and there is no violence in ordinary life."[25] Later she wrote, "I am still slightly puzzled by all this *deus ex machina*—Perhaps I am still too afraid of blood to write of it—perhaps I know nothing of it."[26]

Eric L. McKitrick at the *Saturday Review of Literature*, however, was ecstatic about the book. "'Talent,' in the case of Virginia Sorensen, seems to amount to more than just that; with her, sheer technical virtuosity is undeniable."[27] And Parke, at the *Times*, conceded that "one cannot find fault with the author's full-blooded descriptions of ranch life or her perceptive, sensitive awareness of the deeps and shallows of human emotions."[28] Many others came through with praise as well. "Thoughtfully written, with a satisfying knowledge of its background and a sure eye for detail," wrote James Hilton for the *New York Herald Tribune*. And then Ben Kartman at the *Chicago Sun*, "Mrs. Sorensen is primarily a storyteller, and a gifted one. *The Neighbors* adds appreciably to her considerable stature as a novelist."[29]

"They are all too good," Virginia enthused.[30]

Colorado author Helen Rich wrote in a letter to Virginia, quoting from *The Neighbors*, "'The racket (of the coyotes) held the sky up.' Gosh, I hated you at that moment. Of course, that is what they do and I'll never never hear a pack again without thinking, gol darn

---

23. "The Neighbors," *Kirkus Reviews*, Aug. 2, 1947, kirkusreviews.com.

24. Andrea Parke, "Colorado Ranchers," *New York Times*, Aug. 31, 1947.

25. Sorensen to Smith, Sep. 3, 1947.

26. Sorensen to Smith, Sep. 4, 1947.

27. Eric L. McKitrick, "Western Clan," *Saturday Review*, August 23, 1947, 16.

28. Andrea Parke, "Colorado Ranchers."

29. Back flap of dust jacket for Virginia Sorensen, *The Proper Gods* (New York: Harcourt, Brace, and Co., 1951).

30. Sorensen to Smith, Sep. 2, 1947.

that Sorensen woman. No, I won't. I'll really bless you for finding those words."[31]

Virginia got some more positive attention when she visited her family in Utah a month after *The Neighbors'* publication. "They invited everybody in town, I think, and for the first time I truly tasted home-town adulation. It was the list in the *Times* that did it—to be on the *Times* list is, of course, something indisputable, even if one does not climb the list."[32] However, "the royalties were more disappointing that I thought possible," Virginia wrote. "One gets illusions of grandeur, I suppose, after a full-page in the Times and four weeks of being on the List there! Ah well—we will learn."[33]

To make up for the lack of royalties, Virginia was submitting short stories to various magazines, but so far had received "only reams of rejections from every quality magazine in the country! Maybe I'll be convinced I am long-winded only."[34] So, naturally, she started work on another novel. "Tomorrow school begins, and I will write Part I, Chapter I, at nine o'clock in the morning," she reported. In a tongue-in-cheek response to the criticisms of her previous two novels, one of the stipulations she had placed on herself was to "deal with inner conflicts and have nobody kill or killed."[35]

Her work was briefly halted by a hospitalization for what she worried might be cancer. But it revealed a new side of Fred that Virginia had not known was there. "He used to seem angry when I was sick, and I understood it was because he was used to leaning up on me and when I was not well I didn't make good leaning. But he doesn't lean now. He takes charge and there is true sympathy. How changed he is! I have loved him so much that the sound of his steps

---

31. Helen Rich to Virginia Sorensen, Virginia Sorensen Papers, MSS 1686, box 3, fd. 8, L. Tom Perry Special Collections, Harold B. Lee Library, Brigham Young University, Provo, Utah.

32. Sorensen to Smith, Sep. 26, 1947. *The Neighbors* was number 15 in the *New York Times* best sellers list September 7 and 14, 1947.

33. Sorensen to Smith, dated Mar. 8, 1947, but much evidence points to its being written in 1948. The full-page ad appeared in the *New York Times Book Review*, Sep. 7, 1947, 15. Also, Virginia may have been talking about something else in this quote, but the *New York Times* best sellers list only features *The Neighbors* for two weeks rather than four: September 7 and 14, 1947.

34. Sorensen to Smith, Sep. 26, 1947.

35. Sorensen to Smith, Sep. 2, 1947.

made me simply hammer all over. … It is a relief to have a real man to love at last. One tires of simply being affectionate to an irate child. And it is a good feeling to do some leaning myself."[36]

Fred's other relationships were not going so well. He was getting into what Virginia described as "the same old martyr-complex" with his superiors at the university. He had joined the Colorado state committee for former vice-president Henry A. Wallace's presidential campaign. Wallace was sometimes regarded as a Communist "fellow traveler," both for the policies he promoted and his unabashed willingness to defy the Jim Crow regime in the South. Some academics who had supported Wallace had lost their posts, and Fred seemed to be daring the Denver University hierarchy to just try it. "So you can see nothing is changed," Virginia sighed. "We probably will leave here this September, for where I have no notion."[37]

Fred was a handsome, intelligent, charismatic man, which helped him land job after job, but he was also, as Virginia described him, "stormy petrol," who, time after time, took what seemed to be a perfect situation and turned it sour. It was sometimes affecting their marriage as well. Still, "It flabbergasts me that anybody who has met Fred does not love him," Virginia wrote. "He is like this old house— he has imperfections but they endear him. His furies make a person of him. He always prickles at the right places."[38]

Despite the uncertainty—or perhaps because of it—Virginia continued to work on her new novel, finishing part three (of six) in late February 1948. She had sent a draft of part one off to Metro-Goldwyn-Mayer to see what its Hollywood possibilities might be but heard back that it had "difficulties for the screen." So, no extra money was coming in. "I'm so tired of this dripping house and not being able to afford symphony tickets and riding No. 8 and seeing the mountains like a misty sort of impossible promise," she lamented.[39]

In August 1948, the Sorensen family was packing up again, bound this time for Auburn, Alabama, where Fred had a new position at the Alabama Polytechnic Institute. The same month, Virginia

36. Sorensen to Smith, Nov. 27, 1947.
37. Sorensen to Smith, Feb. 23, 1948.
38. Sorensen to Smith, Nov. 14, 1952.
39. Sorensen to Smith, Feb. 23, 1948.

finished up her novel and sent it off to Harcourt, Brace, and Company.[40] "I felt that I must put it in shape before starting the new life," she wrote. "Now that it is in a piece, whole for me, I am beginning to believe in the book, as I did when it was only the first idea."[41]

When they arrived in Auburn, they moved "way out in the country in a lovely white house on a red hill with sloping grass," Virginia effused. "And below us, down the road about a block, is one of the prettiest little lakes you ever saw. ... We have exquisite woods behind the house and to the east; I look out of my window at the pines and oaks all day."[42]

While Fred ran the freshman English program, Virginia taught creative writing, made possible in part by her new "Westinghouse electric stove which will even cook my whole dinner by oven while I'm off teaching."

Family life had shifted, too. Beth "goes to dancing, to Young People's Night ... to Girl Scouts ... to piano lessons on the campus, to football games where she shouts like mad for Auburn High! Freddie is in the Boy's Choir at the Episcopal Church and loves it—can you imagine?" Beth and Freddie "stay out together until around eleven every Friday, which is an amazing development—Fred and me sitting home waiting until the kids come in!" Sometimes, she wrote, "I stop suddenly in the middle of a good day and think, Surely not! There must be a great big fly in the ointment somewhere! But we can't find any so far."

Soon she received a package from Denmark—a Danish translation of *On This Star*. And her latest novel was well on its way, too. Her editor wrote that he was "much excited with the new book and it needs no rewriting at all, simply some strategic cutting."[43]

After that strategic cutting, *The Evening and the Morning* was published on April 22, 1949. The critical response was positive. "The experience of reading her new book is that of having lived

40. Harcourt, Brace and Co. had acquired Reynal and Hitchcock. "I must have been listed with the liabilities," Virginia quipped in a letter to Linda Sillitoe. See Sillitoe, foreword to *The Evening and the Morning*, by Virginia Sorensen (Salt Lake City: Signature Books, 1999), vi.

41. Sorensen to Smith, Aug. 25, 1948.

42. Sorensen to Smith, Oct. 5, 1948.

43. Sorensen to Smith, Oct. 5, 1948.

with people—and people who disturbingly, inexorably, through all their diversity and complexity, are yourself," wrote an awed Dale L. Morgan for the *Saturday Review*. "That is the power and beauty of this novel, that somehow or other it is everybody's autobiography."[44] From Ruth Page's perspective at the *New York Times*, "This is the story of woman's problems, and the greatest of these is love." And not just love, but "the power of physical love and … the effects of religious dogma when it denies physical love."[45] Even the Provo *Daily Herald* in Utah got in on the action. "Virginia Eggertsen Sorensen has reached a new height of achievement in her new book," wrote Dorothy O. Rea. "Mrs. Sorensen, still in her thirties, writes with skill of the very inner thoughts of child, adolescent and young woman. … The surprising element is the ease with which she grasps the backward glances of those ripe with years."[46]

Then, the cherry on top. "Virginia Sorensen alone has managed to write a completely Mormon novel where the characters are in an important sense truly independent of the background," wrote Fawn M. Brodie, author of *No Man Knows My History: The Life of Joseph Smith*. "The setting is authentic contemporary Mormon but the greatness of this novel is not the least dependent upon it. This is a rare accomplishment."[47]

None of them compared *The Evening and the Morning* to her first book. Virginia had finally broken the *Angels* barrier.

---

44. Dale L. Morgan, "Fruits of Rebellion," *Saturday Review*, Apr. 23, 1949, 13.

45. Ruth Page, "A Woman's Lot," *New York Times*, Apr. 24, 1949.

46. Dorothy O. Rea, "Former Springville Woman's 4th Novel Is Vivid Portrayal of Mormon Life," *Daily Herald*, Apr. 22, 1949, 10.

47. This quote is taken from a typed card that attributes it to *Frontier Magazine*. See the Virginia Sorensen Papers, MSS 1686, box 5, fd. 13, Perry Special Collections. A handwritten note by Mary Kenyon (a researcher helping with the collection of Virginia's memories during the last year of her life) reads, "Virginia said this is probably the best review she ever had."

CHAPTER FOUR

SHE DIVERSIFIES

"I have four novels I want to do almost equally just now," Virginia wrote on July 1, 1949. "Once more my critical approval is on the side of all right, sales on the side of negative, which adds up, for me, to another try in another direction."[1] That other direction proved to be a novel about the Yaqui people in Mexico. It was not the most exciting news her publishers had ever heard. Selling books about Native Americans was hard enough; how were they supposed to find an American market for a novel about *Mexican* Indians?[2] But Virginia had fallen in love with the Yaqui during her trip to Sonora, Mexico, when she was researching the Samuel Brannan book, and she had gone back during her last year in Denver to gather more experience with them.

Writing such a novel was a daunting task that would involve a great deal of research and synthesis. Virginia described the book as "what-the-hell a novelist does to the painstaking facts gathered by cultural anthropologists in the pueblo of Potam in the Province of Sonora, Mexico." Fortunately, two cultural anthropologists who had spent years with the Yaqui, Edward "Ned" and Rosamond "Roz" Spicer, were eager to help her. In a way, it was like the Brannan

---

1. Virginia Sorensen to Anna Marie Smith, July 1, 1949, Anna Marie Smith Papers, MS 540, fd. 12, Merrill-Cazier Library, Special Collections and Archives Division, Utah State University. Unless otherwise noted, all correspondence between Sorensen and Smith is from Smith's papers.

2. Colorado author Helen Rich had the opposite reaction. "I cannot quite tell you of the feeling of thirst I have—thinking about your book. But thirst is the word for it and I think being thirsty to read another's book is quite something. I wonder what kind of drinking this one will be." Helen Rich to Virginia Sorensen, Feb. 28 (no year), Virginia Sorensen Collection, MSS 1686, box 3, fd. 8, L. Tom Perry Special Collections, Harold B. Lee Library, Brigham Young University, Provo, Utah.

project: Ned Spicer was writing an anthropological study while Virginia was writing a novel. "His the fact, mine the fancy, he says."[3] Virginia's novel may have been a fulfillment of Ned's special attachment to the Yaqui. "On the surface [Ned's] writing about [the Yaqui] may appear detached and analytical," Roz wrote in *People of Pascua*, "but back of it is a depth of feeling and a warmth of understanding. Had Ned written this as a novel, there would be more of a development of characters."[4] That character development was just what Virginia was providing.

"Never have I had such a good time at a typewriter!" Virginia wrote. Part of the fun was finding a unique direction to take the story. "I abandoned the original Spicer conception of the hero—the rebel who ends in the gutter," which she felt was a plot "ignobly repeating [itself] in the Departments of English." She wanted her hero to walk "another sort of straight-and-narrow." It would be "a much more subtle tragedy, to my mind."[5] The approach was her own rebellion against current writing trends. She said of many of her contemporaries that "Instead of endlessly winding through complex motivations and characters, they can simply throw lightning down. ... to wipe out anybody or anything that gets out of hand."

By May 1950, Virginia was "polishing off the 389th page" of the manuscript, "and have a little over a hundred pages to go before the 1st of June, when I am to get it off to Spicer who has the time in June to be sure the facts are right."[6] On March 23, 1951, *The Proper Gods*, depicting a young Yaqui man as he tries to integrate with traditional Yaqui culture, was published by Harcourt, Brace and Co.

"One never becomes accustomed to the silence after a book comes out," Virginia wrote in May, a few months after publication, "there is always the belief, carefully hidden, that surely this one is so wonderful, at least here and there, and is so true that people must see it and speak of it together."[7] But the *New York Times* completely overlooked

---

3. Sorensen to Smith, May 17, 1950.

4. Rosamond B. Spicer, "Living in Pascua: Looking Back Fifty Years," in Edward H. Spicer, *People of Pascua*, ed. Kathleen M. Sands and Rosamond B. Spicer (Tucson: University of Arizona Press, 1988), xli.

5. Sorensen to Smith, May 17, 1950.

6. Sorensen to Smith, May 17, 1950.

7. Sorensen to Smith, May 2, 1951.

the book, as did the *Saturday Review*. Kirkus was on top of things, though, and noted that *The Proper Gods* was "wholly different from her previous novels ... and displays almost encyclopedic information about the Yaquis. ... Perhaps more limited in appeal than her other books, this is however a serious and sympathetic appraisal."[8]

Finally, in June 1951, Orville Prescot at the *New York Times* apologized for missing *The Proper Gods* in the "competition of the spring's high tide of new books," and delivered a review. "Mrs. Sorensen's understanding of the Yaqui is nothing short of phenomenal," he wrote. But "there are many times ... when Mrs. Sorensen seems more interested in educating her readers than in entertaining them."[9]

Despite such a lukewarm reception, Virginia remembered the book fondly later in life. "She enjoyed rereading this work, because, as she says, 'it seems to me, to be not bad writing,'" wrote Jacqueline C. Barnes.[10]

Just before she sent her Yaqui novel off to Ned Spicer, a new idea had sneaked into Virginia's head—one that would affect her writing career profoundly. "A bunch of Montgomery [librarians] came to my autographing party in Montgomery last April," she wrote to Anna Marie, a librarian herself. "They had an idea: why didn't I write a juvenile. ... about bookmobiles, and what they do for people."[11] The idea immediately appealed to her because "the greatest shock I received [in the Deep South] was the discovery that a library does not necessarily 'come with a town.'"[12]

In March 1952, she wrote, "I start riding bookmobiles next week in dead earnest. Montgomery next Wednesday, Huntsville the next week, Mobile the week after that. I've got a nice plot worked up and some characters that are beginning to be people inside of my head, mumbling all kinds of lovely folksy things."

Her travels resulted in an article for the *New York Herald Tribune*.

8. "The Proper Gods," *Kirkus Reviews*, Mar. 1, 1951, kirkusreviews.com.

9. Orville Prescott, "Books of the Times," *New York Times*, June 26, 1951.

10. Jacqueline C. Barnes, "Sacrifice to the Proper Gods," *Association for Mormon Letters Annual, 1994* (Salt Lake City: n.p.), 1:78.

11. Bookmobiles are trucks or vans outfitted to carry books and provide library services to underserved areas such as rural locations and retirement homes.

12. Virginia Sorensen, "The Books Were Waiting," *National Parent-Teacher*, Sep. 1958, 33.

"Lately I've been riding bookmobiles through the pine-woods country, along the red Alabama roads," she wrote. "We stop at places like Bigbee's Postoffice, Tibbie's Store, French's Gin." She described one stop on "Mrs. Scott's Lawn, and the sides of the truck were barely down when women and children began coming from up and down the road. ... [A] boy hopped up on the shelf that opened down from the primers and story books, and there he sat for the next half-hour, absorbed in 'choosing.'" She told about "country storekeepers [who] have become neighborhood librarians;" of children who taught their grandmother to read using the bookmobile's primer collection; and of "an old colored man" who came to see if the bookmobile had Shakespeare. They handed a copy to him. "He took the book with reverent hands. 'I haven't had Shakespeare on the place since my cabin burnt down,' he said. 'It's been years now. I was startin' to lose my quotations.'"[13]

She felt like Professor Mifflin in one of her favorite childhood books, *Parnassus on Wheels*, as he drove his travelling bookstore through the countryside. "He knew [books] were not meant to gather dust on Parnassus, but were for the service of men. ... Books are meant to bring strangers together."[14]

"When the writing began to happen, it felt good," Virginia reflected later. "I liked its reality, its solid, useful feel, just as I had always liked making bread, hanging clothes on the line, putting fruit into jars against the winter."[15]

Before she could finish the manuscript, the Sorensen family moved again. Virginia took the blame this time. "I've had the old nose back, each year worse, and this year it has taken the flesh the way it did in California. ... I kept trying to work and falling in a heap. ... Fred and I are going to apply seriously wherever the climate seems feasible."[16] And that place turned out to be the State Teachers College in Edinboro, Pennsylvania.

---

13. Virginia Sorensen, "Where Old, Young, Men, Women, and Children Starve for Books," *New York Herald Tribune,* June 29, 1952, 2.

14. Virginia Sorensen, "The Books Were Waiting," *National Parent-Teacher*, Sep. 1958, 33.

15. Virginia Sorensen, "Newbery Award Acceptance," *The Horn Book Magazine* 33, no. 4 (Aug. 1957): 283.

16. Sorensen to Smith, Dec. 3, 1951.

"We live in a little house on a hill above Edinboro Lake, which is a lake real and big enough to have sailboats and long windings through wooded hills. How I love it after that heavy air and the bare red earth with the ragged pineywoods!"[17]

With her nose returned to normal, Virginia finished up her bookmobile manuscript and sent it off to Harcourt. "It is cursed with my old problems—slowness of getting underway—but really comes to something before the end! ... Montgomery County Bookmobile lady, Ethel Sanders, who became a close friend of mine ... wept tears of pleasure (so she wrote) over my little Alabama Missie, even in that first version!"[18]

Meanwhile, Virginia was at work on another novel for adults, though it had a rough start. "Last year I didn't do anything fit for paper, and am now working on the novel again, having ripped it all to h---! Nothing about it satisfied me, and I can't imagine Harcourt paying me the advance on it as it stood." Like *The Proper Gods*, this new novel drew on Virginia's skills as an amateur anthropologist, but this time she was studying "Utah medicinal lore."[19]

But the children's book market had its hooks in her, and it was not about to let go. Scribner's contacted her to write a young adult novel for a series called *Strength of the Union*. "They offered me Utah or Colorado and I did hesitate, but decided where my real loyalty lies." Utah, of course. The focus of the story was to be Utah's statehood and, "What a subject for a juvenile ... polygamy!"[20]

Virginia's first children's novel, titled *Curious Missie*, following the adventures of an elementary school girl in rural Alabama as she works to bring a bookmobile to the area, was published September 4, 1953. Kirkus called it "perhaps too idealistic in tone but the combination of serious and adventuresome material has value."[21] Two months later, the *New York Times* dubbed it, "genuine" and "well-written."[22] Best of

---

17. Sorensen to Smith, Sep. 12, 1952.
18. Sorensen to Smith, Sep. 12, 1952.
19. Sorensen to Smith, Oct. 19, 1952.
20. Sorensen to Smith, Oct. 19, 1952.
21. "Curious Missie," *Kirkus Reviews*, Sep. 1, 1953, kirkusreviews.com.
22. Sarah Chokla Gross, "Alabama Jubilee," *New York Times*, Nov. 15, 1953.

all, Virginia's daughter, Beth, who was heading off to college, "could at last read a book of mine with unqualified approval."[23]

It was *Curious Missie* that kept Virginia's spirits afloat as she struggled with "the terrible exodus and drain" of her latest novel for adults, now titled *Many Heavens*. It had left her "in a terrific slump. ... No writing at all—only staring and wondering and wishing I had never got into this wild project [the Utah statehood juvenile novel]."[24]

Meanwhile, she had discovered a whole new world in the children's literature speaking circuit. "What a Book Week!" she wrote to Anna Marie. "I talked to about 2000 kids, all told. I loved them all, from First to Ninth. Their good faces and lovely questions and it was the first time in all my life I felt Really Famous!"[25] Another event sent her home "so excited and pleased with the experience that Fred was amazed—I wonder why authors bother to talk to grown-up audiences."[26]

The difficulties of writing *Many Heavens* bore fruit in August of 1953 when Virginia's editor suggested only "'small cuts [that] could be attended to in the galleys,' ... Imagine!"[27] But Virginia had recently run across some historical information that she wanted to integrate. She even liked the painting that would adorn the book jacket, though it was "scarcely Utahn."[28]

Despite Virginia's tinkering, *Many Heavens* came out right on time, February 17, 1954, telling the story of a young woman in Cache Valley, Utah, only a few years after the 1890 Manifesto ostensibly ending polygamy, falling in love with a married doctor while pursuing her own medical career.

"Virginia Sorensen's best novel of Mormon life," Kirkus trumpeted, "even though the solutions she offers may disturb many readers."[29] Oliver LaFarge at the *Saturday Review* wrote, "Virginia Sorensen's full-bodied novel, 'Many Heavens,' is a real technical

---

23. Sorensen, "Newbery Award Acceptance," 278. A much younger Beth had excoriated Virginia when some kittens had died in *A Little Lower than the Angels*. See Virginia Sorensen, "Newbery Award Acceptance," 277.
24. Sorensen to Smith, Dec. 3, 1953.
25. Sorensen to Smith, Dec. 3, 1953.
26. Sorensen to Smith, Aug. 15, 1953.
27. Sorensen to Smith, Aug. 15, 1953.
28. Sorensen to Smith, Dec. 3, 1953.
29. "Many Heavens," *Kirkus Reviews*, Feb. 1, 1954, kirkusreviews.com.

achievement. She has written a novel of character … without letting the setting run away with the story, without triteness, and without lag."[30] Then Andrea Parke at the *New York Times* wrote that Virginia had "made a real tour de force of her material—right down to a happy ending that seems believable because of the simplicity and understatement of the narrative."[31] Virginia was excited to receive a letter from acclaimed sculptor Mahonri Young, a grandson of Brigham Young, saying that "he had just read [*Many Heavens*] and that it was 'completely truthful—too truthful to be popular with the faithful.'"[32]

The House Next Door, Virginia's juvenile novel about Utah statehood, came out the summer of the same year from Scribner's.[33] Meant for a teen audience, it tells the story of Gerry, a girl from Virginia, who lives for a summer next door to a polygamous Mormon family in Salt Lake City. Kirkus called it "one of the better titles" in the *Strength of the Union* series. "While some of the boy-meets-girl aspects are a bit contrived to highlight both sides, the friendship between Gerry and Millie, of the Mormon family, is very well handled."[34] Ellen Lewis Buell at the *New York Times* noted that "The life typified by a Mormon family, which includes three wives and unnumbered children, is sympathetically sketched."[35]

It had been a successful year for Virginia, providing her the resources to go on a trip that would alter the course of her life.

---

30. Oliver LaFarge, "Prophet's Progeny," *Saturday Review*, Mar. 27, 1954, 16.

31. Andrea Parke, "Mormon's Dilemma," *New York Times*, Feb. 21, 1954.

32. Sorensen to Smith, July 22, 1954.

33. She did not care much for the cover, but the art was featured in the collection of *New York Times* children's books reviews *The House Next Door* appeared in.

34. "The House Next Door," *Kirkus Reviews*, June 15, 1954, kirkusreviews.com.

35. Ellen Lewis Buell, "New Books for Young Readers," *New York Times*, Feb. 13, 1955.

CHAPTER FIVE

SHE TRAVELS ... AND MEETS ALEC

"We arrived in [Edinboro] Pennsylvania in September [1952],"
Virginia wrote, "and enjoyed passionately what happened almost at
once to the maple trees. That breathless, unbelievable inner light!"
Autumn soon turned into a long, cold winter. But one day late in
February, the head of the college's art department, whom they called
Pop, took Virginia and Fred out "to see what was going on in the
sugar bush." Virginia was amazed. "Here spring could actually be
seen and smelled and tasted, rising out of the ground."

Soon, Virginia and Fred were exploring the awakening countryside and becoming friends with a "huge Pennsylvania Dutchman
and his wife" who showed them their "sugar camp"—the place where
they made maple syrup each spring. The next year, Virginia herself
"heaved buckets full of sap in the raw cold air," getting to know both
the process and the people involved with "sugaring." A story started
forming in her head.[1]

She brought a draft of it with her for a two-month stay at the
MacDowell Colony, an artist residency program in Peterborough,
New Hampshire, in the summer of 1954. She finished the "maple
story in a few weeks." The characters seemed to match, one-for-one,
the people she had gotten to know in Edinboro.

As a "lovely bonus," she also wrote a short novel set in an Amish
community, which she called "Plain Girl." She described it as
"pure poetry in its own way and probably not for kids."[2] It was this

1. Virginia Sorensen, "Newbery Award Acceptance," *Horn Book Magazine* 33, no. 4
(Aug. 1957): 279–80.

2. Virginia Sorensen to Anna Marie Smith, July 22, 1954, Anna Marie Smith Papers, MS 540, fd. 12, Merrill-Cazier Library, Special Collections and Archives Division,

manuscript that she brought the farthest—"polished like a light."[3] The story idea came from two newspaper articles: one about an Amish father who was arrested for refusing to send his children to public school, another about how two girls, one of them Amish, had traded clothes at school.

One evening at MacDowell, as Virginia was talking with author Carl Carmer, "I tried to tell Carl ... how it felt to be a little Mormon and about that old murder over water," and Hollis Alpert, fiction editor for the *New Yorker*, "said suddenly, 'Will you do that for the *New Yorker*?'"[4] So, by the end of her stay, Virginia had also written a short story. It was a very productive two months for her.

Another resident at the time was fifty-six-year-old British author Alec Waugh,[5] who was working on what would become his best-known novel, *Island in the Sun*. In his memoirs, *The Best Wine Last*, Waugh describes the moment he first saw Virginia, "Beside [the driver] was sitting what looked like a youngish woman.[6] I could not see her face, only the back of her neck. It sent a shiver along my nerves." He talked with her that evening. "She was so happy to be here, to have these two months to concentrate upon her writing. From what private problems she was escaping I did not know, as yet."[7]

The problem Alec sensed was the mounting conflict between Virginia and Fred. Alec blames part of it on the continuing influence of Mother Sorensen, but also because Fred "wanted to write and could not"[8] and because "he was exasperated by the fact that his wife wrote novels that were published and praised."[9] Fred's alcohol use also contributed to their troubles. One can find hints of these

---

Utah State University, Logan. Unless otherwise noted, all correspondence between Sorensen and Smith is from the Smith Papers.

3. Sorensen to Smith, Aug. 22, 1954.

4. Sorensen to Smith, Aug. 27, 1954.

5. A prolific author, Alec is nonetheless best known today as the brother of novelist Evelyn Waugh.

6. Virginia was forty-two at the time.

7. Alec Waugh, *The Best Wine Last: An Autobiography Through the Years, 1932–1969* (London: Allen, 1978), 264.

8. Indeed, Fred had finished a novel, but had a hard time getting even his "best friend" Hubert Smith (Anna Marie's husband) to read it. Sorensen to Smith, Jan. 15, 1954. Waugh did say, however, that Fred "wrote some quite graceful verses," some of which appeared in the *Western Humanities Review*.

9. Waugh, *Best Wine Last*, 265.

conflicts in Virginia's letters, but they always cut off quickly. Two years earlier, for example, Virginia had written, "To have survived at all is a miracle—I mean, of course, the two of us together. I will one day write of these things. It is strange I have not yet."[10] However, during her stay at MacDowell, she wrote that she missed "my Friedrich every day—and every night."[11]

As Alec wrote, after Virginia's first conversation with him, "as she walked back to Colony Hall, she seemed to be floating down the path. 'Steady,' I warned myself. 'Steady. These two months are all important for her. ... You must not spoil it.' ... I submitted to that virtuous resolve for sixteen days."[12]

Indeed, as Virginia wrote to Anna Marie, one day "there was a letter in my door in [Alec's] exquisite handwriting. ... He finished his new novel yesterday at 9:38, he says, and will I share a bottle of champaigne [sic] at lunch! Will I!"[13] The pair got on famously, and Alec extended his stay for a week. By the time the two finally parted (Fred and Freddie picking Virginia up for a trip with Beth to New York), they had made plans to meet up in Denmark, where Virginia would be visiting on a Guggenheim grant to research a new novel.

The seed for this novel was planted by William Mulder, who was writing his dissertation at Harvard about the narratives of early Danish Mormon converts as they trekked to Utah. Having Danish Mormon ancestors on both sides and growing up in the largely Danish-settled community of Manti, Utah, Virginia "wanted to create imaginatively what *might have happened* ... those particular Europeans who came to a particular America for a particular faith," she wrote. "What they abandoned for it is the beginning of the story and that is what I want to go and find out about."[14] With access to Mulder's collections and translations, Virginia was finally ready to tackle the project.

Mulder was excited. "I'm afraid I don't have enough priesthood to issue a call, but ... you must and you will produce that immigrant novel," he wrote to her in 1954. "I am going to send you a

---

10. Sorensen to Smith, Oct. 19, 1952.
11. Sorensen to Smith, July 2, 1954.
12. Waugh, *Best Wine Last*, 264.
13. Sorensen to Smith, July 22, 1954.
14. Sorensen to Smith, Oct. 26, 1954.

list of those stories, diaries, journals, and biographies which I have found rewarding."[15]

As she prepared to go to Denmark, Virginia sent her "Plain Girl" manuscript in to Margaret McElderry, her editor at Harcourt, who, according to Virginia, praised it as "'one for the ages'—'so nearly perfect it might as well be absolutely perfect.' So, of course, she sends two pages of 'suggested revisions.'"[16] Virginia had also read the first chapter to a fourth-grade class; they wrote to her later, saying, "We do not want you to leave out a single word."[17]

Her previous two novels, *Many Heavens* and *Curious Missie,* had both sold very well. As her agent said to her, "I didn't get the breakdown, so I don't know how much is Many Heavens and how much Curious Missie, but what the hell do we care?"[18] And, as a cherry on top, the short story she had written for the *New Yorker,* "Where Nothing Is Long Ago," was accepted.[19]

As her departure neared, Virginia's excitement ratcheted up.[20] "I just want to see what [Denmark] looks like and sounds like and smells like," she wrote. "It has been so many years coming and means so much to me I am sometimes frightened."[21]

The trip, however, had created tension between her and Fred. "I can't mention any of the joy of going because of how Fred feels. He doesn't try to disguise it in the least and periodically makes me feel that I simply cannot leave." But the difficulties between the two had become so pronounced that "I can't *not* leave now or I shall not be able to stay with him anyhow."[22]

---

15. William Mulder to Virginia Sorensen, Feb. 2, 1954. Virginia Sorensen Collection, MSS 1686, box 3, fd. 4, L. Tom Perry Special Collections, Harold B. Lee Library, Brigham Young University, Provo, Utah. At the time, Mulder was compiling a collection of Mormon documents, with A. Russell Mortensen, that would later be published by Alfred A. Knopf as *Among the Mormons: Historic Accounts by Contemporary Observers* (1958).

16. Sorensen to Smith, Oct. 14, 1954.

17. Sorensen to Smith, Oct. 14, 1954.

18. Sorensen to Smith, Oct. 14, 1954.

19. When it came out, in 1955, Mulder wrote to her, "*The New Yorker* seems like such an unlikely place to come upon a Sanpete farmer. Perhaps your story will jar it out of its sophisticated clichés and return it to life. Baptism by irrigation water." Mulder to Sorensen, Nov. 18, 1955, Virginia Sorensen Papers, MSS 1686, box 3, fd. 4.

20. Beth was twenty and Freddie eighteen by this time.

21. Sorensen to Smith, Oct. 14, 1954.

22. Sorensen to Smith, Oct. 14, 1954.

So she sailed for Denmark in mid-December. "I adored the gales, much to the disgust of my tablemates, but it was because I loved everything. The great sea fascinated me endlessly, and I walked the deck for many hours, sometimes under moon and stars after breakfast, for we were very far north—sailed up around Scotland."[23] She arrived in Copenhagen on December 19, the next day writing pages and pages of descriptions of her hotel, the harbor, the shops, the streets, and everything else she saw.[24]

The next morning, she went to the American embassy and, to her delight, discovered that its little library had *The Neighbors* and *The Evening and the Morning*. Then some LDS missionaries met her "and blessed me for the success of my journeys. I was much touched; they were lovely lovely boys. … but what they shall do for the little Finns with their reindeer herds I can't imagine."[25] She spent Christmas with some Britons she had met, talked to some Danish publishers (whose offices Virginia swore were larger and more stylishly appointed than Knopf and Harcourt put together), then went to a New Year celebration where she learned that "one really has to watch out for Danish beer. I've a head [hangover] today."[26]

Already she had started work, going through "whole rosters of shiploads of immigrants, the most marvelous names and incidents."[27] She was also writing an initial draft of another short story for the *New Yorker* that she was calling "The Darling Lady." But she did not stay in Copenhagen for long, heading sixty miles west to Slagelse for a few days, and then three weeks in Jutland, just over a hundred miles still farther west, where she was plied with so much rich Danish food that by the end of the month "I now can't get my green skirt on any longer and the blue one is very tight. … I feel like a balloon tied in the middle."[28]

By February, she was back in Copenhagen where, she wrote, "the

23. Sorensen to Smith, Jan. 1, 1955.

24. Virginia wrote many detailed letters addressed generally to friends and family on Hotel Codan stationery from various locations in Denmark. These are cited as Codan Letters and are found in the Virginia Sorensen Collection, MSS 1686, box 5, fd. 1.

25. Codan Letters, Dec. 20, 1954.

26. Codan Letters, Jan. 1, 1955.

27. Codan Letters, Dec. 28, 1954.

28. Codan Letters, Jan. 24, 1955. "Typical Danish food," according to Virginia, is "much and good."

days are long and quiet and full of me-reciting-Danish-lessons-aloud-in-my-room, practicing on the waitress at each meal." But she was also "reading the new things Bill Mulder has sent. Heavens, I've a bunch of his things now that stand two inches high—and on onion-skin too."[29] Soon she had access to the Royal Library and was reading a microfilm copy of a daybook "written by one of the few sailors to join the Mormon Church. ... I have come to the place where he himself is a missionary, in the West Zealand Country, near Slagelse, where all the Sorensens lived. I read how he converted and baptized 'a young girl, 18 years old, by the name of Sophie Sorensen.'"[30]

The story consumed her for days. "My Danish journal is breaking my heart. I have my hero married now to his beloved Katrine ... and they have left [Copenhagen] and are having a hell of a time getting across all those plains to Zion. ... I get so interested in the journal I forget to write and have to go back again and again."[31] She followed the little family to Fort Ephraim, Utah, where, on "Oct. 15, 1865, they were out digging potatoes one fine day and Indians came and killed them ... left the baby alive, lying in the field. I was weeping into the machinery ... What a saga! The son who survived by a whim of Black Hawk's, translated his father's journal at the age of 91, by dictation to his own son in Salt Lake. I cannot tell you how moved I am by this."[32]

In early February, Virginia noted in a letter home that "[Alec] Waugh is lecturing at the British Center on Tuesday night, so of course shall go."[33] Her letters during her time in Denmark mention Alec infrequently, but, according to Alec's memoirs, they spent so much time together that Virginia took to calling that period "our lit-tle marriage." "We usually supped at the Codan. We kept a bottle of Aquavit [distilled drink] on the ledge between the double windows and ordered up beer and open sandwiches. Then we read poetry to one another."[34]

---

29. Codan Letters, "Monday afternoon" (probably Feb. 7, 1955). "Onionskin" is very thin paper.

30. Virginia read a few days later "that Miss Sophie Sorensen ... was reported ex-communicated for being a whore!" Codan Letters, Feb. 15, 1955.

31. Codan Letters, Feb. 14, 1955.

32. Codan Letters, Feb. 15, 1955.

33. Codan Letters, Feb. 12, 1955.

34. Waugh, *Best Wine Last*, 271.

It was not unusual for men to fall in love with Virginia. In letters dated March 12, 1944, and January 11, 1945, to Anna Marie, Virginia talks about men who expressed their unreciprocated infatuations with her in one way or another. But it seems that with Alec the attraction was mutual. Whether Virginia and Alec's relationship progressed beyond poetry during this period isn't documented.[35]

But whatever Virginia was feeling for, or doing with, Alec, her physical distance from Fred seemed to be improving her relationship with him—something she very much wanted. They exchanged some intimate and conciliatory correspondence in February. "Your letters are very beautiful and very profound and—as none were last summer—full of love," she wrote to him. "I'm sorry I hurt you, for I didn't mean to do it. Perhaps my going on and on about doing this and that is hard for you to bear when I thought it would make you happy. ... [But] you felt left out, especially since the accident of fortune has given me something so truly splendid and so dreamed of. Yet I constantly think we will yet share such things, and that it will make us new again, together."[36] Soon she was making plans to bring Fred to Denmark someday. "It will be worth it to you when it happens and I show you these streets and canals and people and towers and all."[37]

These letters, however, were also filled with worries about money: what money was coming in (not much), what money was going out (too much), how to pay taxes (quarterly), how to keep track of expenses

---

35. Decades later Virginia gave a hint about her relationship with Alec at the time in a cassette tape recording she made in Tangier, "I have just come through July ... 1984, with all of our celebrations; it was July 1 when [Alec and I] met; July 8—[Alec's] birthday; July 15 we were married; the 17th we always celebrated as the anniversary of the first night we spent together. See "Virginia Sorensen Waugh's cassette, Side 'B'," transcript by Mary Kenyon, p. 1, Virginia Sorensen Collection, MSS 1686, box 8, fd. 5, L. Tom Perry Special Collections, Harold B. Lee Library, Brigham Young University, Provo, Utah. This makes it possible that Virginia and Alec spent their first night together (which could indicate any number of scenarios) while at MacDowell Colony, since Alec says in *The Best Wine Last* that he kept his promise to stay away from Virginia for sixteen days (and since they met on July 1, the July 17 date matches perfectly). But according to Virginia's extant letters to Anna Marie, her first significant contact with Alec at MacDowell Colony (the bottle of champagne to celebrate finishing his novel) was on July 22, 1954 (five days after July 17). If the landmark night didn't happen at MacDowell, it also didn't happen during her European tour, since it ran between December 1954 and May 1955.

36. Codan Letters, Feb. 19, 1955.

37. Codan Letters, Feb. 28, 1955.

(in great detail), where Virginia should stay (at a less expensive hotel). All this because a Fulbright grant Virginia had been pursuing had not materialized, and *The House Next Door* was "selling badly on account of polygamy. Lots of raised eyebrows—and U. of Utah has refused to speak of it to the Scribner's district manager for the Education department. So no royalties from there—apparently in the red."[38]

Despite the bleak financial outlook, Virginia was being encouraged by Anna Marie and Alec to tour Europe while she had the chance. Alec, she reported, "said if it was only money that prevented me from seeing something while I was here it was nothing but damn foolishness."[39] He said she could come to Nice, southeastern France, and do some typing for him to finance her tour. Besides, Virginia told herself, "It is an investment, I can't go on pulling books out of my little life on my Western halfacre—can I?"[40] Fortunately, Naomi Burton,[41] Virginia's agent, was able to persuade Harcourt to pay Virginia's royalties sooner, making her tour a possibility.

On April 1, 1955, Virginia took a train to Odense, Denmark, where "Great Grandfather Eggertsen was born!" There, she participated in a Hans Christian Andersen festival.[42] During one event, she sat in a balcony seat opposite the king. "Saw him blow his nose and all," she wrote.[43]

Soon she was on her way to Paris. "I am glad I saw Copenhagen first, for after Paris I think all cities must be somehow pale," she wrote as she went on a whirlwind tour. "If I sound breathless, I am."[44]

Then it was on to Nice, which she dubbed "more wonderful still."[45] There she was introduced to Alec's extensive social circle and started typing his memoirs, including his "memories of Hugh Wal-

---

38. Codan Letters, Mar. 11, 1955.

39. Codan Letters, Mar. 19, 1955.

40. Codan Letters, Mar. 19, 1955.

41. Naomi Burton was also literary agent to Thomas Merton, Ogden Nash, and Ian Fleming.

42. She was also gathering material for a book about Hans Christian Andersen she had titled "The Most Amazing Thing."

43. Virginia continued to write detailed letters to friends and family during her European tour. These are found in the Virginia Sorensen Papers, MSS 1686, box 5, fd. 2, and are cited as Europe Letters. This one was dated Apr. 1, 1955.

44. Europe Letters, Apr. 5, 1955.

45. Europe Letters, Apr. 9, 1955.

pole and Edmund Gosse. … It is fascinating stuff—since his father was a publisher he met most of the great people of that whole era."[46] She also got a peek into life in the bigger literary pond. "[Alec] has just had news from New York that his huge novel 'The Sugar Barons' will run in *Ladies Home Journal* for five issues. He says he hasn't made 'that many thousands' since he sold a movie … Well, it is another world, isn't it? … He tells everybody about my books—almost embarrassing, for of course they listen politely and then must ask what on earth Mormons are."[47]

She also started to understand Alec's lifestyle, so different from her own. "It's interesting to catch a glimpse of the wandering hotel-existence Alec has—'resident alien' is a good name for him and nothing else would suit him at all. He has little nests of friends all over the world and says he is always feeling that he is both coming home and going away, his notion of an ideal combination. … Of all odd things, he's rather religious and wouldn't miss church for anything. Doesn't matter what church—but apparently this keeps him feeling rooted as much as he needs to be."[48]

Most alien of all, she encountered her first bidet. "Did I tell you about the strange and wonderful little French things in the hotels. … It's rather like a long slim toilet but is always there besides the toilet and is simply for washing bottoms in a good sensible sitting position."[49]

The trip was doing her some good. In mid-April, she was "excursioning to Italy" where she had a hair-do mishap. But then she had someone fix it into "rather a frank and downright poodle! … I've never been so pleased with my hair in my whole life! It's lovely when I go to sleep and lovely when I wake up again."[50] She had also managed to lose all the weight she had gained in Jutland, "So much that my jeans hang like a sack … I've not been so thin since the Neighbors came out, and really rather like it."[51]

By this time, she was starting to miss her life back home and

46. Europe Letters, Apr. 9, 1955.
47. Europe Letters, Apr. 9, 1955.
48. Europe Letters, "Day After Easter" [Apr. 10, 1955].
49. Europe Letters, Apr. 12, 1955.
50. Europe Letters, Apr. 18, 1955.
51. Europe Letters, Apr. 21, 1955.

realized that she was "having qualms about having deserted the nest for a while."[52] Alec tried to persuade her to join him at a PEN[53] conference in Vienna, but, as he observed, "She had problems to be settled [at home]. Her children needed her."[54] So, after a tour through Brussels, Hamburg, and some final days in Denmark, she sailed for the United States on May 25, 1955. Her time in Europe had lasted six months.

"When I left," Virginia wrote of Dr. Ingeborg Boberg, who had helped her so much in the folklore collection at the Royal Library in Copenhagen, she had felt "unable to thank her adequately[. She] laughed at my attempt and said, 'It is only a good exchange. You will return to us all we have to give to you—but in one book!'"[55]

Virginia headed home to write that book—which would actually turn out to be two books. But she would not complete either until after the highest point of her career and the lowest point of her marriage.

---

52. Europe Letters, Apr. 21, 1955.

53. PEN (now called PEN International), a worldwide association of writers, was originally an acronym for Poets, Essayists, Novelists.

54. Waugh, *Best Wine Last*, 272.

55. Virginia Sorensen, "World in a Closet," *Utah Library Association Newsletter*, Spring 1956, 6.

CHAPTER SIX

HER BEST AND WORST YEARS

Plain Girl, portraying the difficulties an Amish girl encounters as she navigates the tension between Amish culture and the public school she is forced to attend, was released September 29, 1955. Despite Virginia's original idea about the book's audience ("probably not for kids"),[1] it turned up under the "For Ages 8 to 12" heading on a *New York Times* summer reading list.[2] In that same newspaper, Rose Friedman praised the novel: "Developing her theme tactfully, her characters perceptively, the author reaches into the heart of Amish life." *Plain Girl* sold well and made its way onto many classroom reading lists. Virginia received student fan mail for decades afterward. Soon, it had won a Child Study Award, boosting its sales and visibility even more.

As *Plain Girl* made its way into the world, Virginia was hard at work on her Denmark novel. "The desire to tell the story I heard so often in [Mormon] Testimony Meeting when I was a child (in that unforgettably delightful accent) has always been with me,"[3] she wrote to Anna Marie Smith. She planned it as the first book of a "trilogy which I am so ready to write it comes from my ears and eyes and fingertips, all together, for I read it aloud and listen and weep

---

1. Virginia Sorensen to Anna Marie Smith, July 22, 1954, Anna Marie Smith Papers, MS 540, fd. 12, Merrill-Cazier Library, Special Collections and Archives Division, Utah State University, Logan. Unless otherwise noted, all correspondence between Sorensen and Smith is from the Smith Papers.

2. "Young Readers' Choice of Books for Summer," *New York Times*, June 3, 1956. In the same category were *Henry Huggins*, by Beverly Cleary; *The Moffats*, by Eleanor Estes; and *Little House in the Big Woods*, by Laura Ingalls Wilder.

3. Sorensen to Smith, Oct. 26, 1954.

and write."[4] She also started work on a juvenile novel set in Denmark called *Lotte's Locket*.

Her relationship with her husband also seemed to be improving. It started with his stepping away from alcohol. "Fred is splendid even though on the water-wagon," Virginia wrote. "Or perhaps I should say because he's on it." And by the end of the year, they had swung into full-blown romance again. "Fred has never been so wonderful. Whatever may be lost, this is vast compensation, and it feels so like a future again. As if we had gone to The [Mormon] Temple and Renewed Our Covenants!"[5] But by February 1956, Virginia was trying to find a summer teaching job for Fred. "Just now keeping him up somehow is my Number One Problem," she wrote to Anna Marie. "Fred does need a change and a rest, poor guy—what an existence, with this damned Professional Woman in the house."[6] There was another cloud on their horizon, as well: "Alec worries Fred," Virginia wrote, "but quite needlessly, as you may imagine." Fred did have some warrant, though; Virginia had, after all, written from Denmark that Alec "is really my idea of a perfect friend"[7] and had met up with him in Cleveland after her Denmark trip in October 1955.[8]

In June 1956, Virginia was back at MacDowell Colony where her writing time and her marriage improved. "Fred sent on a wonderful poem today. Funny—he never agrees that I'm bad for him, yet the moment I'm out of sight he does these exquisite things. As much as I love him, I'm afraid I really drain him dry. Maybe I should say *because* I so dearly love him."[9]

But she also dearly loved writing.

Writing every day no matter what is the only answer as far as I can see— and the resentment I feel when I *can't* spend part of each day writing

4. Sorensen to Smith, "Labor Day" 1955 [Sep. 5, 1955].

5. Sorensen to Smith, Nov. 21, 1955. She was referring to the LDS temple marriage covenants, a curious reference considering how far out of the church she and Fred were. But her LDS heritage was much on her mind as she worked on her Danish novel.

6. Sorensen to Smith, Feb. 10, 1956.

7. Europe Letters, Apr. 12, 1955, Virginia Sorensen Papers, MSS 1686, box 5, fd. 2, L. Tom Perry Special Collections, Harold B. Lee Library, Brigham Young University, Provo, Utah.

8. Alec Waugh, *The Best Wine Last: An Autobiography Through the Years, 1932–1969* (London: Allen, 1978), 284.

9. Sorensen to Smith, June 15, 1956.

is very real and deep, in a way the deepest and realest emotion I have, after love. So you see—the curse is that I love working and cannot do without it. So if it tires me, what of that? So does love. So does a grand walk. So do all the things that matter. If one gives nothing to them one gets nothing back, they don't count at all.[10]

The second of the two books Virginia produced at MacDowell in 1954, *Miracles on Maple Hill*, came out on August 26, 1956. It told the story of a young girl spending a year in the Pennsylvania countryside and learning about sugaring, but, as *Kirkus Reviews* pointed out, it also carried a "theme not too often examined in children's books nor nearly so well done as it is here,"[11] namely, post-traumatic stress disorder[12] in returning soldiers. "Warm and real as Mrs. Sorensen's two previous books centering about a 10-year-old … this one is packed with incident, country magic, family love and people to remember; it has substance and spiritual worth," said the *New York Times*.[13]

Soon after the publication of *Miracles*, Virginia's daughter, Beth, married. "They seem very happy," Virginia wrote, in contrast to her own marital feelings. In December 1956, she flew to Tucson and met with Alec. "We had an idyllic time, in the mornings drinking mint juleps by the swimming pool," Alec wrote.[14] But the trip weighed heavily on Virginia. Again, her relationship with Fred was on the rocks. "I had to make up my mind whether I wanted to be a worldly cosmopolitan or not," she wrote. "I love Alec very much and I love his life too—the Spicers[15] had dinner with him and me and were in on all this Big Decision, strangely enough." But in the end, "I decided to stay with Fred, finally and irrevocably."[16]

Three months later, "the sky fell in."

"Since the … 4th of March, everybody has been asking, 'How does it feel to receive the Newbery Medal?'" Virginia said in her Newbery acceptance speech for *Miracles on Maple Hill*. "The truth

---

10. Sorensen to Smith, June 15, 1956.
11. "Miracle on Maple Hill," *Kirkus Reviews*, Aug. 1, 1956, kirkusreviews.com.
12. Though that diagnosis had not been developed yet.
13. Sarah Chokla Gross, "Country Magic," *New York Times*, Aug. 26, 1956.
14. Waugh, *Best Wine Last*, 284.
15. The anthropologists who had helped her with *The Proper Gods*.
16. Sorensen to Smith, Dec. 29, 1956.

is that I've been wondering ... how joy could be so solemn, how a feeling of new courage could have so much fear in it, how I could feel at the same time so exalted and so humble."[17] She attributed the success of her story to the "fact that it has the most ancient theme in the world, the recurrent pleasures, the rhythms of existence that we human beings are privileged to observe, if we will."[18]

"I was in New York from Sunday to Friday," she wrote to Anna Marie, "the [award] ceremony, signing books, attending parties, sessions on the novel, lunches, dinners, [the Broadway musical] *My Fair Lady* ... It was all wonderful and I'm still so tired I can hardly write this letter."[19] "As you know, [Fred's] contribution to everything I ever did is beyond measure. Now, after nearly 25 years of a marriage with few dull moments, our companionship is the most honest, sympathetic, real thing in the world, so re-awakened and substantial that I feel as if I were in the land of beginning again."[20]

With the Newbery Medal came a flurry of invitations to speak across the nation: Kansas City to Salt Lake City to Boulder, Colorado, just to begin.

When the whirlwind was over at the end of the year, Virginia wrote to Anna Marie.

> Wasn't it my year and everything, full of splendors? And it was, yes, even in September, with Fred seeming rested and satisfied. Then October. Suddenly he began to be different. Bought guns. Went hunting constantly, early and late. Took up smoking big cigars. Began insisting he was A Man. Not Mr. Virginia S, mind you, carrying suitcases. ... And not Professor, either, any longer. In November he suddenly resigned to be A Writer.
>
> Each time a book came out, I was always punished in some way, and apparently the Newbery demanded something absolutely final and sufficient. He says himself it is as if he must blot me out—and he wants me to leave. But where, how? Of course it is old and involved and there is the strong flavor of all that alcohol in it, and Ma S is there ... and Authority.[21]

---

17. Virginia Sorensen, "Newbery Award Acceptance," *Horn Book Magazine* 33, no. 4 (Aug. 1957): 275. Privately she admitted to Anna Marie, "I didn't weep—I simply wanted to shout and laugh and instead of doing either I got down to work on the novel because my agent called." Sorensen to Smith, Mar. 11, 1957.

18. Sorensen, "Newbery Award Acceptance," 284.

19. Sorensen to Smith, Mar. 11, 1957.

20. Sorensen to Smith, Apr. 26, 1957.

21. Sorensen to Smith, Jan. 8, 1958.

The increasing strife destroyed Virginia's ability to write. "Here in the fine wind of opportunity I become a rock and cannot move. ... *Lotte* simply folded up and became meaningless."[22] Then her Danish novel was "first swollen out of proportion and then stopping short, short of the end."[23]

In February 1958, Virginia moved in with her brother Paul for a while in Texas "to try to recover a little and also face the realities of the situation. Fred kept wanting me to go, saying he would be better and calmer if I were gone."[24] While she was there, Fred got into "an accident with a borrowed car," probably precipitated by a mix of alcohol and a manic phase he was cycling through, which helped convince him to admit himself to a mental hospital.[25] This threw Virginia into a "tailspin,"[26] and soon she was back in Edinboro with Fred and Mother Sorensen. When Virginia's son, Freddie, heard that she and Fred "must stay together a while," he wrote back, "Two people who should never have met."[27]

When Fred emerged from treatment, Virginia helped him look for a new job, which "at Fred's age and rank is a miserable business."[28] She was also looking for a way to get them to Denmark, having learned from Alec how to write off her travel expenses. Her efforts paid off: they spent part of the summer in Europe, Freddie even joining them for ten days. When they returned, Fred had a job in New Jersey. "Please cross your fingers and say a prayer that we will find some sort of peace there, some sort of newness or oldness, *something*," she wrote to Anna Marie in August 1958.[29]

Any peace they found did not last long. Toward the end of October, Virginia wrote to Alec saying that "she had finally and definitely left [Fred]."[30] To Anna Marie, she wrote, "I simply cannot tell you what happened that made me have to take [this step]. I only say that

---

22. Sorensen to Smith, Jan. 8, 1958.
23. Sorensen to Smith, Mar. 25, 1958.
24. Sorensen to Smith, Feb. 3, 1958.
25. Mary Lythgoe Bradford, "Virginia Eggertsen Sorensen Waugh," in *Worth Their Salt, Too*, ed. Colleen Whitley (Logan: Utah State University Press, 2000), 196.
26. Sorensen to Smith, Feb. 3, 1958.
27. Sorensen to Smith, Mar. 25, 1958.
28. Sorensen to Smith, June 9, 1958.
29. Sorensen to Smith, "Last of August" 1958 [Aug. 31].
30. Waugh, *Best Wine Last*, 285.

I am glad to be alive and that I discovered I very much wanted to live."[31] Reportedly, Fred had tried to strangle Virginia.[32]

"[Brother] Paul says I was all too slow at taking that 'great big scary step,'" Virginia wrote. "Now it is taken, though one foot remains in the air (if not *both*) and I must begin slowly to walk along again."[33] The divorce was finalized on December 28, 1958,[34] but Virginia continued to keep tabs on Fred. Even a year later she wrote, "How can one get over someone who has been that close for that long?"[35] She also had a difficult time extracting herself from Mother Sorensen. "How she destroys me—one sees and feels her plucking every string of dread and guilt. ... She has helped me to understand one emotion I always doubted—pure unadulterated hate. She is like a vampire greedy for the marrow of one's bones."[36]

When March 1959 came around, after some time at MacDowell, Virginia finally sent her Danish novel off to Harcourt, her editor replying that "cutting is going to be difficult, if only for the reason that everything in the book is a pleasure to read."[37] Newly unencumbered, a book delivered, a check cashed, and embarking on a year of travel, Virginia felt "frighteningly happy now. It is hard for me to believe in thoroughly good things. ... Perhaps it is time I should be 'cherished and loved and spoiled somewhat'—as Alec says it."[38]

---

31. Sorensen to Smith, Oct. 31 [no year].
32. Bradford, "Virginia Eggertsen Sorensen Waugh," 196.
33. Sorensen to Smith, Oct. 22, 1958.
34. Sorensen to Smith, Jan. 14, 1960.
35. Sorensen to Smith, Jan. 14, 1960.
36. Sorensen to Smith, Nov. 20, 1959.
37. Sorensen to Smith, Apr. 7, 1959.
38. Sorensen to Smith, Apr. 7, 1959.

CHAPTER SEVEN

HER CAREER ENDS ... AND IS REMEMBERED

Beginning in early 1959, Virginia and Alec used her new freedom to visit together places all over the world—the West Indies, Europe, Morocco, Ireland, the Ivory Coast, Singapore, and Cambodia, among others. "The succession of departures and reunions maintained the spirit of romance between Virginia and myself," Alec wrote.[1] Despite the romance, Virginia seemed to have no further designs on Alec. "As soon as the divorce was final ... I knew I didn't want to be married any more. Especially not to Alec, for I love him so very much for his freedom."[2] Alec was actually married and had been the entire time Virginia had known him. But he was amicably estranged from his wife, Joan Chirnside, their relationship being conducted largely through letters. Virginia said that Alec considered himself a kind of "Wandering Romeo."[3]

Some writing projects were nagging at Virginia, including *Lotte's Locket*, which she had been working on for four years, and a book about Hans Christian Andersen, for which she had signed a contract. Soon she would take on a nonfiction project about Danish Americans.

Her Danish novel, *Kingdom Come*, was released March 16, 1960. Chad Walsh, at the *Saturday Review,* said, "The qualities that make it very good indeed are its warmth, its delicate understanding of love,

---

1. Alec Waugh, *The Best Wine Last: An Autobiography Through the Years, 1932–1969* (London: Allen, 1978), 286.

2. Virginia Sorensen to Anna Marie Smith, Jan. 14, 1960, Anna Marie Smith Papers, MS 540, fd. 12, Merrill-Cazier Library, Special Collections and Archives Division, Utah State University, Logan. Unless otherwise noted, all correspondence between Sorensen and Smith is from the Smith Papers.

3. Sorensen to Smith, Mar. 2, 1962.

[and] its unobtrusive but sure craftsmanship."[4] But apparently the readers of 1960 were not looking for a "leisurely novel" about Mormon converts in nineteenth-century Denmark. In April a disheartened Virginia wrote that not even members of her family had bought copies, "They 'wait to borrow Dad's!' ... Infuriating."[5] And then in May, "I've had the customary sad letter from my editor—'we all feel very sorry here that the book has not had the great success we all hoped for.'"[6] Since *Kingdom Come* was supposed to be the first part of a trilogy, "I dread coming to Volume 3 with Volume 1 already out of print!"[7]

Virginia continued to travel, deliver lectures, take up visiting writer positions, and became a grandmother to Beth's daughter Susan. She and Alec set up a "three months' experiment with house-keeping in Nice [France]," but the experience convinced Virginia that she still did not want to marry him. Alec, too, "never expected 'our affair' to last." But on the other hand, he "prayed that it would last as long as possible."[8]

Halfway through 1960, from a cottage in Devon, England, Virginia wrote bemusedly, "I don't seem to want to write very much when I'm happy!"[9] But Alec pushed, telling her she "must do my [Danish] Saga to the bitter end."[10]

In June 1962, Virginia drove to Springville, Utah, where she lived with her father for several months. Virginia's sister Helen had died recently, and it had taken a terrible toll on him. He also had an aneurysm, which could cut his life short at any time. Alec joined them for two months, becoming friends with her father. While there, Virginia wrote some short stories that drew on the same childhood memories she had based her previously published short stories on.[11] On September 7, her son, Freddie, got married—by a Mormon ward bishop,

---

4. Chad Walsh, "The Conflicts of a Quiet World," *Saturday Review*, Apr. 16, 1960, 26.

5. Sorensen to Smith, Apr. 4, 1960.

6. Sorensen to Smith, May 25, 1960. Though she did sell 10,000 copies, according to William Mulder, "History, Memory, and Imagination in Virginia Eggertsen Sorensen's *Kingdom Come*," *Dialogue: A Journal of Mormon Thought* 35, no. 1 (Spring 2002): 98.

7. Sorensen to Smith, May 25, 1960.

8. Waugh, *Best Wine Last*, 287.

9. Sorensen to Smith, July 1960.

10. Sorensen to Smith, Mar. 2, 1962.

11. The stories included "Where Nothing Is Long Ago" and "The Face" in the *New Yorker*, and "The Other Woman" in *Story* magazine.

no less.[12] And in the spring of 1963, Virginia delivered the story collection to her publishers in New York "about two hours before my ship sailed."[13]

The collection, titled *Where Nothing Is Long Ago: Memories of a Mormon Childhood*, was released the summer of 1963. In the *New York Times* Fawn M. Brodie wrote, "No one sees better than [Virginia] the hidden wealth in [Mormonism's] cloistered, parochial community, abounding in love and little miracles."[14] *Kirkus Reviews* said that "the local color ranges from striking to dazzling."[15] The collection has since become one of Virginia's most enduring books in LDS circles.

That left Virginia with the Hans Christian Andersen book, "due (and of course years *past* due) by the end of September [1964]," and the Danish American book, due Christmas. "Then I'll be free of this damn burden I permitted myself to take on. … Work goes so very slowly now, any work at all; age, of course,[16] and perhaps a kind of lethargy that comes from wondering whether it all matters much."[17] Virginia got a reprieve when the Andersen book's editor moved to another publishing house, but she doubted she would hit even the new target date. "I no longer meet deadlines or accept them or think of them—impossible, so why pretend?"[18]

She was right. She never did finish the Andersen book, the Danish American book, or the other two parts of the *Kingdom Come* trilogy.

But she did finally deliver *Lotte's Locket* to the publisher. "I didn't even do the final copy—girls at the office did," Virginia admitted. "Otherwise I should never have had the strength. Writing is unbelievably difficult now. … I apparently can't make it a total way of life, as Alec can."[19] The novel was published October 7, 1964. "The story is primarily interesting for its portrayal of Copenhagen and the Danish country village." wrote *Kirkus Reviews*. "The description of

12. Sorensen to Smith, Aug. 1962.

13. Sorensen to Smith, Mar. 7, 1963.

14. Fawn M. Brodie, "Of Saints and Sinners," *New York Times*, Sep. 15, 1963.

15. "Where Nothing Is Long Ago: Memories of a Mormon Childhood," *Kirkus Reviews*, June 15, 1963.

16. She was fifty-two years old.

17. Sorensen to Smith, Aug. 10, 1964.

18. Sorensen to Smith, Sep. 28, 1964.

19. Sorensen to Smith, Sep. 28, 1964.

[Lotte's] eventual recognition of the need to be with her mother and new father is incomplete and unsatisfactory."[20]

Soon, the marriage and health of Freddie broke down, and he began living with his mother in her home in Alexandria, Virginia—a stay that would last two years. "It was the first time that they had been alone together," Alec wrote. "He and Virginia … found that they had a great deal in common," including a love of poetry.[21] When Freddie recovered, he began working as a hospital orderly. Alec himself stayed with Virginia from time to time in a "carriage house that Virginia had fixed up" that included a studio, a shower, and a kitchenette.[22]

It was during one of his stays in 1968, as he worked on a book about Bangkok, that Alec received word that his wife of the past thirty-six years, Joan Chirnside, was dying of throat cancer. He flew immediately to England. Though Alec and Joan had been married for three and a half decades and had three children together, they rarely saw each other.[23] "What are your plans?" she asked him when he arrived. "It was a question that I was not ready to answer yet," Alec realized.[24] She died within a few days; Alec attended her funeral.

"The next day I returned to the US," Alec wrote. "I knew now the answer to Joan's question 'What are *you* going to do?' I went straight to Alexandria. Virginia was sitting by her fire. I sat beside her. 'I hope,' I said, 'that you'll agree that after a proper and appropriate interval we should get married.'"[25]

The couple married on July 15, 1969, at the Rock of Gibraltar. Alec was seventy-one, Virginia fifty-seven.[26] Their "little marriage" was starting to become a big one.[27]

The newlyweds moved out of the hotel they had frequented in

20. "Lotte's Locket," *Kirkus Reviews*, Oct. 1, 1964, kirkusreviews.com.

21. Waugh, *Best Wine Last*, 301.

22. Waugh, *Best Wine Last*, 301.

23. "Joan was a wonderful correspondent," Alec wrote. "She had written to me every five days or so and had told me what [the children] were doing week by week in a way that their occasional letters in the future could never do." Waugh, *Best Wine Last*, 306.

24. Waugh, *Best Wine Last*, 303.

25. Waugh, *Best Wine Last*, 307.

26. "Alec Waugh, 71, Marries Virginia Sorensen, Author," *New York Times*, July 17, 1969, 58.

27. At Alec's request, Virginia also converted to Anglicanism in 1977. Mary Lythgoe Bradford, "Virginia Sorensen," *Sunstone*, Feb. 1992, 17.

Tangier, Morocco, and set up house in the same city, which was their main base of operation for eleven years. With her new last name, Virginia started feeling increased pressure to write. "I have come into a long literary tradition and now have the name and feel obliged to do justice to it ... so I am writing again, very hard, very seriously. ... If I don't write now I am hopeless."[28]

She indeed had a book in the works, which she called "The Boy Who Went Around the Corner," "about Alexandria and a Negro family and a West Virginia family that is indigent because of the mines and all that." It was a story that she thought "was as good as Plain Girl."[29]

She was also starting into another book that she called "a campus novel, somebody going back after ten years—after twenty-five years as a faculty wife. It is good to write from memory now and not to look anything up."[30]

Many months after sending "The Boy Who Went Around the Corner" to the publisher, however, she still had not heard back. "I polished it off, really polished!—and find myself a bit tense about it. It's very different, larger than I thought, might not even be for children, I'm not sure. I need to be told!"[31]

When she did finally hear back, her editor "wanted some changes I couldn't seem to make. ... She thinks it isn't 'abrasive' enough for the new children—it is too 'sweet and light.'"[32]

The title shortened to *Around the Corner*, the book came out October 27, 1971. It was about a young Black boy living in a "barely middle class neighborhood" who is told by his mother to stay away from a transient (and white) family that has taken temporary residence in an abandoned house around the corner. *Kirkus Reviews* noted that the characters talk about "a wide range of right-on topics—race relations, living close to nature, and women's lib. ... Though the conflicts are worked out with improbable ease and the

---

28. Sorensen to Smith, Dec. 6, 1969.
29. Sorensen to Smith, Aug. 12, 1969.
30. Sorensen to Smith, Sep. 23, 1970.
31. Sorensen to Smith, Sep. 23, 1970.
32. Sorensen to Smith, Dec. 28, 1970.

propaganda is a little thick at times, the sharp characterization and convincing dialogue lend an air of credibility."[33]

The audience Virginia really wanted to impress, though, was her grand-daughter Susan, to whom she had dedicated the book: "Remembering the fun we had reading this story, chapter by chapter as it was written." But when Virginia visited her, Susan forgot to mention the book at all. "Her enthusiasm was for the story of a young would-be suicide and her experience in the hospital, called *I Never Promised You a Rose Garden*. She and her 11-year-old friends were exchanging paperbacks of this sort as we used to exchange the adventures of Campfire Girls. I feel my little story will never be heard of again. I am so hopelessly out of touch with America and its children."[34]

She took comfort in her "campus novel," which was going "well but very slowly."[35] "I painstakingly try to perfect each line, each page, as if I were writing a sonnet instead of a novel. And the next day it seems wrong again. Like a disease. But what truly marvelous hours I have had living with these characters."[36]

A year later, in 1973, Virginia delivered the novel and reported that Harcourt "seems enthusiastic" about it. She, on the other hand, felt "only cautious and slightly hopeful. The main thing is that I finished it."[37]

All her time living in Tangier and interacting with the Americans and Britons residing there (usually as government personnel) and their children had led Virginia to start writing another juvenile novel, which she called "Companions of the Road." "I really feel ready to do this one now. Everything blooms around me when I begin to work—Morocco becomes home."[38]

The "campus novel," titled *The Man with the Key*, was released April 17, 1974. It followed the story of a newly widowed forty-ish faculty wife who has an affair with a Black man, and the trouble it starts at the college. *Kirkus Reviews* was unimpressed, categorizing

---

33. "Around the Corner," *Kirkus Reviews*, Oct. 1, 1971, kirkusreviews.com.
34. Sorensen to Smith, Dec. 28, 1971.
35. Sorensen to Smith, Aug. 16, 1972.
36. Sorensen to Smith, Dec. 21, 1972.
37. Sorensen to Smith, Sep. 29, 1973.
38. Sorensen to Smith, Sep. 29, 1973.

the novel as "for mature, womanly, garden club readers who may enjoy all the phlox but then they might not like … the rather determinedly Modern middle-aged sex."[39]

A month later, Virginia wrote disconsolately to Anna Marie Smith, "No word from any of my friends and relations about the book—one wonders if they are embarrassed, quite helplessly!"[40] Ten years later, she admitted that "it seemed to me it had fallen dead from the press—not a word from a soul, and my 'friend' Lily came to the door with an author's copy, there in Tangier, and said, 'Here—your book will not fit with your other books on my shelf!'"[41]

"The only cure for one book is another," Virginia wrote, and she started in earnest on "Companions of the Road," which she had high hopes for. "If I do no more books for children, which seems likely at this moment, I feel that this one is … a splendid finale."[42] She wrote the book while a stuffed lamb doll sat on her desk, a symbol of Boots, the lamb her protagonist keeps as a pet during the story.

When she sent the manuscript off, her editor, Margaret McElderry, wrote back saying that the book would not be illustrated—the first time this had happened to one of Virginia's juvenile novels. "She says that illustrations price books out of the market, even the library market, which is the greatest part, of course," Virginia sighed. "Anyhow, we will have a colorful Moroccan jacket."[43]

By this time, Virginia was starting to feel her age (sixty-five), including "various pressures on the nerves causing eye trouble, stiff neck, dizziness, imbalance, double vision and all sorts of assorted emotions." It turned out that she had "a giant aneurism in my poor old dizzy head."[44] Alec's health was starting to flag as well, and Virginia's daughter, Beth, had recently gone through a divorce.

And then the "Companions of the Road" galleys came. "I sent them back the other day," Virginia wrote, disheartened, "it's not a

---

39. "The Man with the Key," *Kirkus Reviews*, Apr. 1, 1974, kirkusreviews.com.

40. Sorensen to Smith, May 17, 1974.

41. Sorensen to Smith, "Christmas Time" 1984. Harcourt did not even advertise the book.

42. Sorensen to Smith, Jan. 1, 1977.

43. Sorensen to Smith, Jan. 1, 1977.

44. Sorensen to Smith, Oct. 18, 1977.

very good book, I'm afraid."[45] Officially titled *Friends of the Road*, it was released March 10, 1978. *Kirkus Reviews* called it "a rather disaffecting story of a self-confessed 'State Department Brat.'"[46] Eight years later, Virginia revised her opinion of the book to "pretty bad."[47]

However, renewed interest in Virginia's early Mormon novels was starting to emerge among LDS scholars. This upsurge was led by Mary Lythgoe Bradford who, on Bill Mulder's suggestion, had written her master's thesis on Virginia's novels in 1956. She had since become the editor of *Dialogue: A Journal of Mormon Thought*, and dedicated part of the Fall 1980 issue to articles about Virginia's novels, as well as an interview and a short story titled "The Depot."

Virginia's marriage to Alec was both balm and burden to her. She completed little writing during her marriage. "It would make him sick to have me say I'd rather cook lunch for him and linger over it than write a story," she wrote nine months before his death. But "one does not complain that one has been too happy these late years! Too absorbed in somebody else's life to care enough about one's own."[48]

In October 1980, with Alec's health failing, Virginia and Alec left Tangier and moved to Tampa, Florida. He had a stroke there and was confined to the hospital for two weeks before dying on September 3, 1981, at age 83. "One day the nurses said I should go and have some lunch while they turned him over," Virginia remembered, some years later. "I came back quickly to find him half turned, and that in the meantime he had ceased to be. I have lived that moment over and over."[49] She took comfort in the fact that "Alec dreaded becoming senile and the old 'club bore.' He didn't wish to live any longer after his physical health failed. ... My last act for him at the end was to speak to him of love, and he, too, through dry lips. And I straightened his eyebrows, lest he open his eyes again and find them in the way."[50]

45. Sorensen to Smith, Oct. 18, 1977.

46. "Friends of the Road," *Kirkus Reviews*, Mar. 1, 1978, kirkusreviews.com.

47. Sorensen to Smith, "Christmas Time" 1984.

48. Sorensen to Smith, Dec. 10, 1980.

49. "Virginia Sorensen Waugh's cassette," transcript by Mary Kenyon, 1, Virginia Sorensen Collection, MSS 1686, box 8, fd. 5, L. Tom Perry Special Collections, Harold B. Lee Library, Brigham Young University, Provo, Utah.

50. "Virginia Sorensen Waugh's cassette, Side 'B'," transcript by Mary Kenyon, 3, Virginia Sorensen Collection, MSS 1686, box 8, fd. 5, L. Tom Perry Special Collections.

Three years later, Virginia reflected, "I had two very good marriages, I thought of calling my memoirs *Twice-upon a Time.* (I had these good men twenty-five years apiece, with a little overlapping in the middle.)"[51]

Virginia hated the humidity and bugs in Florida. So she, Beth, and Freddie moved to Hendersonville, North Carolina, where she settled in a house with a hill behind it.

She desperately wanted to write. "But I have been wandering around in the house, on the hill, through the long days, doing nothing at all! Or very little. Aching with the neuralgia left by the nerve-cell damage ... by the shingles—the pain is still acute and chronic."[52] She would compare herself to Alec, who "wrote every day until he woke with his hand immovable."[53] "Alec kept saying, 'I have written everything I know, but you have barely started on your material and experience ...' I ask his busy spirit to forgive me. There is simply too much."[54] "I no longer learn easily ... events, like dates, run together like mixed fruit in juices—a splendid, confused concoction of jumbled colors, tastes, and fragrances—very inviting, wanting to be written down like sausage, and heather."[55]

"I feel a great flood of remorse and sadness when I think of my failures," Virginia wrote to Bill Mulder a few months before her death, "especially that I abandoned the *Kingdom Come* trilogy. I was troubled that KC was never translated and published in Denmark, and of course felt that it was not good enough."[56]

Aging was simultaneously fascinating and frustrating for Virginia:

---

51. "Opening Remarks," *Exponent II* 10 no. 2 (Winter 1984): 3. Later she recorded onto a cassette tape, "I have never ... written anything about the end of my marriage to the father of my children, because I was afraid (even though they knew all about it, of course) that it might cause them suffering to have *other* people know." "Virginia Sorensen Waugh's cassette," 7–8. The little I was able to find about the events leading up to the disintegration of her marriage to Fred came from bits and pieces of her letters, most of which are included in this book.

52. Sorensen to Smith, "Christmastime" 1984.

53. Mary Kenyon, "Tues., May 29, 1990, Conversation w/ Va. Sorensen," 1, Virginia Sorensen Collection, MSS 1686, box 8, fd. 5.

54. Sorensen to Smith, Apr. 16, 1985.

55. "Virginia Sorensen Waugh's cassette," 3–4.

56. Quoted in William Mulder, "History, Memory, and Imagination in Virginia Eggertsen Sorensen's *Kingdom Come*," *Dialogue: A Journal of Mormon Thought* 35, no. 1 (Spring 2002): 98.

"It all wants saying but I've no energy to say it, so now I know why it has been so seldom said well, and seldom said at all. Such a universal experience so hidden by the ones who live it."[57]

Toward the end of her life, a flood of attention came Virginia's way. In 1989, the Association for Mormon Letters held a conference at Weber State College in Ogden, Utah, focusing on Virginia's works, which she attended. "I found an amazing number of fans out there," she wrote, "and it seems to me they all want to start a correspondence."[58]

Then, in 1990, Dennis Rowley, curator of the literary archives at Brigham Young University, received a fellowship to "conduct oral history interviews with her to provide a base document for [her] memoirs ... possibly to be published ... as a 'conversations' type of book."[59] Mary Kenyon conducted the interviews during the summer of 1990, also writing descriptions of Virginia's furnishings, bookshelf contents, and daily life. Sadly, Rowley died in 1996 before completing the project.[60]

Virginia knew at the end of her life that she had not been entirely forgotten. Many of her papers had been archived at Boston University and at BYU. And, before the end of the decade, plans would be underway to reprint some of her Mormon books, including *A Little Lower than the Angels* (Signature Books, 1997), *Where Nothing Is Long Ago* (Signature Books, 1998), and *The Evening and the Morning* (Signature Books, 1999).

On December 24, 1991, Virginia Eggertsen Sorensen Waugh died of cancer. She was seventy-nine.

57. Sorensen to Smith, Apr. 16, 1985.

58. Sorensen to Smith, Dec. 31, 1988.

59. Dennis Rowley to Charles Redd Center, no date, Virginia Sorensen Collection, MSS 1686, box 9, fd. 9.

60. The documents can be found in Virginia Sorensen Collection, MSS 1686, box 9, fd. 9, L. Tom Perry Special Collections.

CHAPTER EIGHT

MORMONISM'S "NEW PIONEERS"

What does it mean to be a member of a lost generation? In the LDS mind, the phrase calls up references in the Book of Mormon to a race of people "dwindling in unbelief" (see, for example, 4 Ne. 1:38). Indeed, that has been how Virginia Sorensen and her literary contemporaries, such as Vardis Fisher (1895–1968) and Maureen Whipple (1903–92), have been viewed: a generation of Mormon writers who published novels that were meant primarily to please the world, not the Mormon community.

The phrase "lost generation" was applied to these writers by Edward A. Geary, a professor of English at Brigham Young University, borrowing it from the larger literary world where it characterized a group of American writers—Ernest Hemingway, Gertrude Stein, F. Scott Fitzgerald, et al.—whose world view and writing were impacted by the horrors of World War I. Many of them self-expatriated to Europe where they produced work that was often critical of their homeland. Mormonism's lost generation looks much the same, its writers leaving Utah and Mormonism to produce works critical of their religious homeland.

However, the novels of Mormonism's "lost generation" heralded a major step forward for the Mormon image in American literature. Until the lost generation started publishing, the Mormons were often cast as the villains when they showed up in popular publications. They were murderous Danites killing apostates, or devious missionaries luring comely young women into polygamy, or wagon-train massacring mobs. Arthur Conan Doyle's first Sherlock Holmes story, *A Study in Scarlet*, featured Mormons as antagonists.

Zane Grey used Mormons as villains in his western dramas. And dime novels, as popular in their day as television series are in ours, could not get enough of bloodthirsty Mormons in their plots. So it was an amazing feat when Virginia Sorensen and her contemporaries presented fully human, sympathetic Mormon characters to the American public. It was a sea change that helped to widen the literary possibilities of Mormon characters in the American mind.

Back in Utah, however, Mormons tended to show little-to-begrudging gratitude for this improvement. In his review of *A Little Lower than the Angels*, LDS apostle John A. Widtsoe damned the book with faint praise in the church's official magazine, *The Improvement Era*, which likely contributed to the novel's dismal Utah sales. Why did Mormonism at large so roundly reject these groundbreaking novels?

It was only a few decades earlier that Mormonism was willing to countenance fiction at all. Brigham Young (1801–77), as he strove to build the Mormon kingdom in the Utah desert, had condemned novel reading as a waste of time.[1]

Though Mormonism had tried to keep itself largely isolated from the rest of the United States, the completion of the transcontinental railroad in 1869 brought the outside world, and its culture, trickling in, with ideas and attitudes that often, it seemed, were not compatible with the system Mormonism had built up. These ideas came in the alluring forms of novels, which used narrative to worm their way into impressionable minds and plant secular seeds. It soon became apparent that instilling the Mormon gospel into the minds of the young through preaching was no longer enough.

In response, future LDS apostle Orson F. Whitney called for what he termed "home literature": fiction written by Mormons for Mormons with the explicit objective of promoting Mormon beliefs and building the LDS kingdom. The church officially got on board in 1889 when B. H. Roberts, a leading church official, published "A Story of Zarahemla" in the church's *The Contributor* magazine.

Home literature borrowed the alluring aspects of "worldly" fiction and filled them with Mormon values and stories: injecting Mormon

---

1. Richard H. Cracroft, "Cows to Milk Instead of Novels to Read: Brigham Young, Novel Reading, and Kingdom Building," *BYU Studies* 40, no. 2 (2001): 102–31.

lifestyles and beliefs with the dramatic flavor young Latter-day Saints were so eagerly lapping up. It was as if LDS writers had beaten devilish swords into celestial plowshares.

Home literature reached a zenith in 1898 with the novel *Added Upon* by Nephi Anderson, which encapsulated the goal home literature was striving for: a story that made dramatic sense of *any* Mormon's life. The book starts in the premortal life where a male and female spirit fall in love and promise to find each other in the next life. By surmounting obstacles and adhering to Mormon principles, they do so, soon returning to the Celestial Kingdom together.[2]

The power of Anderson's story structure is that it gives the reader a strong narrative to impress upon their own lives, beginning with a heroic first act that explains how they arrived in their current situation and what it means, followed by promises of a glorious third act predicated on the choices they make now—in the second act. If readers make wise choices, they themselves can follow this story to its happy ending. Nothing is left to chance. The story is clear, the path is marked, the conclusion is certain.

This idea, that a narrative can provide an unerring pattern for the reader's life, was central to Mormonism's origins. The Book of Mormon's main theme is that if you are righteous, God will prosper you in the land, but if you are wicked, you will be swept off. But instead of showing the happy ending, the Book of Mormon shows the tragic ending. Hundreds of thousands of people die because they do not follow the path laid out for them. And if we have learned anything from the history of literature, it is that tragedies make deepest impressions, both on the personal and cultural psyches. Think *Hamlet*, *Death of a Salesman*, *West Side Story*, ... and the Book of Mormon.

Almost every story in the Book of Mormon explicitly illustrates this single theme and allows for no deviation. Indeed, the first metaphor the Book of Mormon presents is a "rod of iron" which safely leads spiritual seekers through a "mist of darkness" to "the tree of life." Anyone who lets go of the iron rod or wanders away from the tree is lost in "forbidden paths."

With such a strong storytelling tradition at the root of the LDS

---

2. Readers may recognize similarities between this plot and that of *Saturday's Warrior*, a musical popular in the 1970s adapted for video in 1989 and film in 2016.

belief system and culture, it was the lost generation's deviation from this pattern that bothered Mormon readers the most.

Sorensen's Mormon protagonists may be found walking various paths of both faith and doubt. In *A Little Lower than the Angels*, Mercy Baker follows her husband into Mormonism, not because she loves its gospel, but because she loves her husband. Chel Bowen in *On This Star* stands firmly on the Mormon path, ready to marry in the temple and have a family, when she begins falling in love with a Jack-Mormon pianist returning to the valley. This pianist, Erik Erikson, though unbelieving, is engaged in a labor of love, weaving together the songs and hymns of Mormonism into an organ solo that makes him a local hero. And in *The Evening and the Morning*, Kate Alexander returns to her Mormon homeland to see if she can reconnect with an old lover and maybe her old religion. Across the ocean in Denmark, Svend Madsen, of *Kingdom Come*, joins the LDS Church, becomes a missionary, and eventually immigrates to Utah with his new wife recently plucked from Lutheranism. In *Many Heavens*, Niels Nielsen walks a razor's edge as he returns to Utah, not as a believer, but as a lover, of Mormonism.

In other words, none of Sorensen's characters travels the sure path laid down by the traditional Mormon story structure. Her stories do not end with her characters either triumphant or destroyed. No particular values are being promoted, and none roundly condemned. Rather, readers are presented human beings trying to make their way through a complex and shifting world with no iron rod in sight.

Apostle John A. Widtsoe articulated the "faithful" Mormon response to Sorensen's work first when he expressed his disappointment that her portrayals of early church leaders seemed to him "ordinary, rather insipid milk and water figures. That does not comport with the historical achievements of the Mormon pioneers."[3]

Widtsoe had a point. The traditional Mormon narrative has power. It propelled thousands of people from New York to Ohio to Missouri to Illinois and across the American plains to Salt Lake City. Its vision gave its adherents the motivation they needed to do the bone-hard work of settling Utah. At the time Widtsoe was

---

3. John A. Widtsoe, "A Little Lower than the Angels," *Improvement Era* 45, no. 6 (June 1942): 380.

writing, the narrative was driving the Saints toward becoming financially and socially successful in mainstream American society. With a narrative that was obviously so productive, what use could a good Mormon possibly have for this alternative story structure—one that seemed to wander without a clear goal, or split off into unknown paths, or dwindle in self-reflective circles? Why would you want your life story to end like one of Virginia Sorensen's novels when you could use Nephi Anderson's ending instead?

Mormons simply could not see the *use* of a Sorensen novel. Besides, what made this writer think that presenting Mormons without their driving story was anything other than a misrepresentation? Since she grew up among the Saints and had no excuse for ignorance, was this a betrayal? Or was she trying, as Richard H. Cracroft contended, "to persuade the readers that true happiness lies not in the sequestered valleys of the West but in the cultural capitals of the world."[4] Either way, the Mormons insisted that she was not doing the world or her religion any favors.

However, this orthodox Mormon interpretation of the lost generation does not take into consideration the monumental changes happening in the LDS Church at the time and how they were affecting its members.

The year 1890, almost twenty-two years prior to Virginia Sorensen's birth, was a turning point in Mormon history: the year Wilford Woodruff, then president of the LDS Church, presented the Woodruff Manifesto, restricting plural marriage and marking the beginning of the LDS Church's long journey toward integration with the United States.

It was a significant turning point because, after Joseph Smith's death in 1844, the Mormons who followed Brigham Young immigrated to the Great Basin beginning in 1847 to escape the United States. Soon the area became part of the U.S. and the Mormons found themselves once again subject to US laws, which later forbad polygamy. That was a problem because polygamy had become a central tenet of the church. Both public opposition and government enforcement grew to the point where Woodruff became convinced

---

4. Richard H. Cracroft, "Seeking 'the Good, the Pure, the Elevating': A Short History of Mormon Fiction, Part 2," *Ensign*, June 1981.

that the church would be destroyed if it did not relinquish this practice. Isolationism was no longer feasible. The only way forward was for the church to succeed on America's terms—to move from black sheep to golden child.

The church had already taken its first public step toward integration when the Mormon Tabernacle Choir won second place in the choir contest at the Worlds' Fair in 1893. It was the first time the American public saw Mormons *being* American—and doing a good job at it. In 1907, Apostle Reed Smoot was allowed to keep his seat in the United States Senate. The church was sending its young people out not just to spread the gospel but to gather knowledge from the universities of the world for Zion's benefit. The story of Mormonism was no longer the one-way story of "gather to Zion," it was now the circular story of "go ye out from Zion and return with riches and knowledge for her benefit."

This shift was in full force when Virginia Sorensen was coming of age. The young Latter-day Saints of that time comprised the avant-garde in this new experiment. They were pioneers, just as their great-grandparents had been, but this new generation was called to synthesize the capitals of culture with the sequestered valleys of Zion.

What would that synthesis look like? No one knew—including these budding writers. It was new territory, and it was not meant to be explored so much as created: one does not write a book the way one settles a frontier community, especially when one is supposed to write that book for everyone. The home literature movement had written only for its own people, the goal being to maintain the Mormon fortress against the onslaught of the world. Now things had changed. Mormonism was conceding that the outside world had value and that it must be integrated with, but how were its members supposed to go about creating that synthesis?

Virginia Sorensen's Mormon novels were about exactly that. Rather than being prescriptive (as her home literature forebears were), her novels are descriptive, showing readers, with great detail and insight, characters navigating the borderlands between Mormonism and the rest of the world. Thus, we have Mercy Baker, in *A Little Lower than the Angels*, with her heart outside Mormonism and her body inside, while Erik Erickson, in *On This Star*, is in the opposite position. There is Kate Alexander, the aging protagonist of *The Evening and the Morning*, who removed herself from her Mormon valley many years ago and then returns to see if there is anything she can reclaim of her past.

Sorensen's characters seem lost and unsure because they had not been prepared for this journey. They are feeling their way along; interacting with the world as they find it; picking up the disparate oddities, tragedies, and treasures they find along the way and trying to make something new out of them. That new thing is either unrecognizable to both Mormons and the world, or it requires a new aesthetic to appreciate.[5] Sorensen's Mormon novels are a series of experiments in integration, all of them emerging with something that has the substance of both Mormonism and the world, but cast in a form that is neither one nor the other.

The difference between home literature and Virginia Sorensen's novels is like the difference between the Old Testament and the New Testament. The Old Testament is about how a peculiar people establishes itself in the world. To do such a thing requires judgment: of how its people behave, of how they think, of what they value, of what they should sacrifice for. The Book of Mormon is largely an Old Testament-style book: its characters punished and rewarded according to their beliefs and actions. They are pawns of the story, being pushed toward redemption or destruction by the theme's invisible current.

If the Old Testament is about how God judges his people, the New Testament is about God's mercy. Just as the central theme of the Four Gospels and Paul's writings is that God's great miracle is coming into atonement with all of creation, so is it in Sorensen's Mormon novels.

An example of this shift between Old and New Testaments, between home literature and Virginia Sorensen, is the New Testament story of the woman caught in adultery. The orthodox members of Jesus' community bring a woman who had clearly broken their law to ascertain Jesus' judgment. Instead of casting judgment, Jesus replies, "He that is without sin among you, let him first cast a stone at her" (John 8:7), pushing the accusers to look within so that they can see the piece

---

5. Such as *wabi-sabi*, a Japanese concept denoting something that is beautiful *because* of its imperfections.

of themselves that is much like the woman. By eschewing judgment, he beckons the accusers, and the accused, toward connection.

Of course, Jesus was not well liked by many in his community. He did not encounter Judaism the way they did, he did not present them to outsiders as they wanted to be presented. His boundaries were sometimes permeable; he could see outsiders too empathetically and insiders too clearly. He had the disconcerting habit of connecting insider and outsider, seeing what new thing would synthesize from that connection.

The Old Testament certainly resonated with the Saints as they trekked into their own wilderness and established their own kingdom. But times were changing. As with the Israelites of Jesus' time, the Mormons were now faced with how to interact with a world that would not let them alone. They could no longer establish themselves purely through power and identity, they must now learn how to connect.

The hallmark of Sorensen's writing, noted repeatedly by reviewers and critics, is her ability to empathize with every one of her characters. Though Sorensen's characters may wander the wilderness of belief, they are not lost, because they are deeply understood and loved, both by the author and, soon enough, by the reader.

It is true that most of the writers categorized in the lost generation did not have Sorensen's powers of empathy and connection. However, they were all on the same journey: trying to bring Mormonism into conversation with the rest of America. All of them tackled the task with their own particular genius. It just so happened that Sorensen took a path of atonement and ushered in the most Christlike novels the Mormon tradition has produced.

Geary's theory of the lost generation provides insight into this group of writers. But I wonder if a more precise term for them would be "new pioneers." It acknowledges the uniqueness of their situation and honors the journey they took into unknown literary territory where they produced some of the best Mormon literature we have today, opening a cultural door between Mormonism and the rest of America (and later the world) that all Latter-day Saints have benefitted from in one form or another. That some of these authors did not return to Mormon orthodoxy is not relevant. Pioneers are not known for returning to their homeland.

CHAPTER NINE

HER NOVELS

A Little Lower than the Angels (1942)

During the 1940s, the first thing most Americans thought of when they heard the word "Mormon" was polygamy. Sorensen took full advantage of that in her first novel, *A Little Lower than the Angels*. But polygamy was just the shiny trinket that drew readers to her book; once inside, they found out that Sorensen was exploring something much larger. Her title, drawn from Psalms (8:5) where the singer praises God for making humanity "a little lower than the angels," may have been warning its readers that the characters in this book would be stretching to bridge that gap between humanity and divinity—not understanding what lies beyond it.

Unlike most frontier towns, Nauvoo, Illinois, was being built communally by a people who believed that the Kingdom of God on Earth looks much different from the Kingdom of Man. This pooling of labor sprang from a spiritual vision. As protagonist Simon Baker puts it, "Nothing should be done that makes the world less a place to love, and nothing should be done that makes a man less than he was before he did it. Because there's one big job to do, and that is to grow."[1] Nauvoo is doing a great job of that. Its citizens talk dismissively of a little startup town north of them called Chicago.

A Mormon family is growing just on the other side of the Mississippi River in Iowa, their tiny house on a bluff that gives them a view of Nauvoo: Mercy and Simon Baker with six children that are about to become seven. But this is not where they had originally

---

1. Virginia Sorensen, *A Little Lower than the Angels* (New York: Alfred A. Knopf, 1942), 192.

planted themselves. Only a little while earlier they had been living in New York. "I didn't want to come," Mercy admits to her friend, the Mormon poet Eliza Snow. "But Simon had to. The Elders came on a Wednesday and by Friday Simon was getting ready to move."[2] Mercy follows him not for love of the gospel, but for love of him. "Nowhere else in the world," but with him "was there a similar peace or a purer one. It had to be made of those who belonged together through the firm right of blood and bones."[3]

Speaking of Eliza Snow, there's something growing in her, too. A love for Joseph Smith, the prophet of this people and the husband of her friend Emma. Already thirty years old, Eliza is unmarried, and though honored in the community for her poems, she feels that her body "has never been really alive or of any use to anyone."[4] After Joseph reveals the doctrine of plural marriage to Eliza and asks her to marry him, she says to Mercy Baker, "It's as though the air touches me all over, as though I breathe through every inch of my body, it's as though I'd just discovered the world and that I was in it."[5]

Growth will push each of them into unprecedented territory, as they all soon find out.

Simon surreptitiously attends an out-of-town meeting about the "Mormon menace" and realizes as he is swept up by the crowd that "these men were afraid of the Mormons, and jealous, too, without knowing it. They didn't trust a community that could grow as Nauvoo was growing, they were afraid of her."[6] Beyond that, rumors of plural marriage among the Mormon leadership had been broadcast by former Nauvoo mayor John Bennett, inciting further antagonism. The Mormons had become too alien to be considered benign. Stretching so far out of accepted norms, they simply did not look human anymore. They looked like a cancer that must be excised.

Eliza walks on air for a while, not even balking at the perfunctory wedding ceremony in a small office followed by Joseph taking up some paperwork and rushing off to a meeting. He tells her he will meet her alone before the next quarter moon, and she awaits him

2. Sorensen, *A Little Lower than the Angels*, 13.
3. Sorensen, *A Little Lower than the Angels*, 124.
4. Sorensen, *A Little Lower than the Angels*, 173.
5. Sorensen, *A Little Lower than the Angels*, 105.
6. Sorensen, *A Little Lower than the Angels*, 204.

anxiously. But Emma finds out about Eliza's marriage to Joseph and their friendship ends.

Adored and hated by so many, and pursued by both, Joseph never visits Eliza. One night she expresses her abject loneliness to him, even admitting her jealousy, and he retorts, "You always understood everything; you could grasp what I meant and put it in forty stanzas of rhymes before the others even got it. And now you're jealous. Like any other stupid ordinary woman!"[7] Soon after this blow to Eliza's soul, Joseph is martyred.

Meanwhile, Mercy bears twins—her eighth and ninth children—and her body finally revolts. She tries to take up her tasks again but suffers fainting spells that incapacitate her. "Something to do with her heart," says a doctor. The family is left without an essential parent, and Simon goes to Brigham Young, the leading member of the Quorum of Twelve Apostles, for advice. Without batting an eye, Young shows Simon to the home of Charlot Leavitt and suggests they marry. At first, Simon is taken aback, but Charlot, a strong-willed, hard-working, religious woman, talks him into it on their way across the river. The ferry captain, a Mormon elder, marries them on the boat, and the two enter the house as man and wife.

Charlot becomes the savior of the household, likely saving Mercy's life and providing months for her to convalesce. The house becomes spotless again, the children overcome bad habits, and Simon has a new wife—though no one knows it yet. When Mercy realizes Charlot's relationship to Simon, her heart breaks. As for the family, "It was as though the circle that had flowed endlessly and easily, the circle that had been a whole and simple thing, had struck an encumbrance and had stopped turning, like a broken hoop."[8]

In the midst of this domestic turmoil, Charlot bears her own child, and "the world was gentler for her and sometimes she even left the dishes on the table long enough to take up her boy and dandle him, singing."[9] Her marriage, so destructive in so many ways, also gave life—to Mercy, to the new baby, and to Charlot's heart.

"It was like being out of the world, out on a star maybe where

---

7. Sorensen, *A Little Lower than the Angels*, 171.
8. Sorensen, *A Little Lower than the Angels*, 338.
9. Sorensen, *A Little Lower than the Angels*, 358.

nothing was the same and you marveled at nothing," thinks Mercy, as she contemplates polygamy. "Everything you had believed, the steady purpose of marriage, the faith and the certainty, it was all gone and you held out your hands and it eluded you."[10] She finally realizes that "nothing then, would be easy and solved, but only on another plane and defined with reference to new conditions."[11] This is the ineffable sphere in which angels tread.

A Little Lower than the Angels is the first example of Sorensen's genius for drawing the tension of situations that, in lesser hands, would be plotted as a battle between good and evil, to the point where the reader can dwell in each character's heart and have the room to watch the consequences of their actions—both terrible and joyful—with a stunned compassion.

On This Star (1946)

When you live in Mormonism, you live in a pattern. It is a pattern that creates a particular sort of person: hardworking, optimistic, obedient, community-oriented. But this pattern seems to work best in isolation, whether physically or psychologically. It flourished in early Utah for a few decades, far away from the rest of the nation. But Utah eventually became a part of the United States, and Mormonism had to change. What that change was supposed to look like, no one knew.

Virginia Sorensen lived in the thick of this change, as unaware as anyone around her how to approach it. What happens when a Mormon emerges from the valleys of Utah into the outside world? What happens when the outside world enters the valleys of Utah—especially when Mormon isolationism had practically been an article of faith up to that point? Mormonism found itself changing little by little each time one of its members left Utah—not to find converts to bring home to Zion, but to establish a new life—and it did not have a way to talk about or incorporate those changes.

Virginia was one of these Saints, emerging from Provo, Utah, relocating to Palo Alto, California, then to Terre Haute, Indiana, then to Denver, Colorado, then to Sonora, Mexico. Her life and faith

---

10. Sorensen, *A Little Lower than the Angels*, 113.
11. Sorensen, *A Little Lower than the Angels*, 334.

changed significantly during those years. But how those changes resonated back in Zion was complicated. What happens when one of these newly cosmopolitan Saints returns to Zion, their worldly patterns coming into sudden contact with Mormonism's isolationist patterns? It was a scenario that had been playing out over and over again ever since the railroad had connected Utah to the rest of the United States in 1869. And it was Sorensen who novelized those fraught returns. *On This Star* was the first of these novels, and the most tragic.

The story is set in Templeton, Utah (based on Manti, Utah), with Chelnicia Bowen (Chel for short), a beautiful early-twenties Mormon woman a few weeks away from marrying a second-generation Danish man, Jens Eriksen. She belongs to the valley, "turned to the contours of this land like the sunshine itself. She was the beginning and the belief."[12]

But her fiancé has a half-brother, Erik, the son of his father's polygamous wife. Erik has returned to Templeton for the summer from the East where he performs as a pianist and organist. He has offered to give Chel, who also plays, lessons as a wedding gift. It is at their first lesson that they meet.

Erik, small and dark, is nothing like Jens, blond and burly. But as Chel listens to Erik perform on the church organ, she is enthralled. The pattern of the music calls out to her. "She knew when there would come a breaking of the order, and when it came, perfect, it leaped in her skin."[13] She is getting her first taste of something other than the Mormon pattern.

Meanwhile, Erik is re-tasting the Mormon pattern, and realizing that, even though he is no longer a practicing Mormon, the church is an essential part of him. One Sunday, as he plays the organ for congregational singing, "on the stool and feeling the keys and hearing the singing behind him, he ... felt a rightness within himself, a sort of stay against confused loneliness."[14] He loves the hymns, he loves the people, he loves the pattern—but he cannot live here, physically or psychologically.

---

12. Virginia Sorensen, *On This Star* (New York: Reynal and Hitchcock, 1946), 27.

13. Sorensen, *On This Star*, 15.

14. Sorensen, *On This Star*, 22.

The pattern, which worked so well for the previous generation, no longer has room for everyone. A family dinner grows tense as Erik insists that those who move out of the valley should not be accused of having "poor ways," and that Templeton children should be taught to *expect* to move out of the valley: "If anything's sure nowadays, it's change," he says.

The idea is tantamount to heresy at the table. "You have to give children the Truth," intones his eldest half-brother, Ivor. "You have to show them the Way."

"All I said was that there are some the pattern doesn't fit," Erik persists.

"Then it's because they pull out of the pattern," Ivor gently rebuts.[15]

So, readers have Chel, born and raised in the Mormon pattern, awakening to a worldly pattern through Erik. And Erik, part of a worldly pattern, but reawakening to his love of the Mormon pattern through Chel. It is the beginning of an enthralling love story.

To fall in love is to be overwhelmed by something beyond oneself. To see the world anew through another person. One of the great gifts of *On This Star* is going on that enthralling journey again with Virginia as guide—re-feeling those ecstasies and agonies in exquisite, poetic (and sometimes bodily) detail.

But in the end, this story is not about the romance between Chel and Erik (it is just the most thrilling part). This story is about what happens when two patterns—embodied in Chel and Erik—converge.

At first, this convergence is wildly productive. Chel sees exciting new possibilities opening up with Erik, with music, and with the larger world. Erik feels his sense of the sacred emerging again through Chel and starts to integrate his music with his Mormonism. Chel comes alive to her body; Erik comes alive to his soul. But the relationship seems doomed, Chel being too much a part of the valley, and Erik too much a part of the world.

"Jens was what she needed," Erik observes one day, "as right as rain for who she was. He saw that clearly. And yet not right at all. He felt a familiar rebellion—the sort of rebellion he felt about a piece of music which failed somewhere in the pattern, which did not reflect

15. Sorensen, *On This Star*, 31.

what came before or prophesy truly what came at the end. ... It was a discord, a raw poor thing which could not be completed in beauty or in satisfaction."[16] He knows that "nobody broke from this sort of permanence, built carefully and determinedly, without suffering. But something outside of the careful structure was taking charge of her as it had taken charge of him."[17]

The alchemy of their relationship culminates in a concert at the church where Chel astonishes the crowd with her performance, and where Erik plays an arrangement of Mormon hymns and folk songs he composed during the summer. As Chel listens, she hears

> the little themes turning into the greater pattern again, almost a marching song, great strides over endless country, a giant striding over mountains. Come ... come ... ye Saints ... He made it strong and deep like mountains and like valleys.
>
> She knew everything he meant.[18]

On This Star comes in two parts. Part I is the love story. Part II is its aftermath. Chel and Erik, once so alive and creative, have become ghosts of themselves. Chel abandons the piano and alienates herself from her family. "There were not many places Chel wished to go, besides those which tasted of duty."[19] Erik makes a marginal, meaningless living with his music, and spends drunken evenings circling philosophical drains. Chel and Erik do not have each other, she having chosen to marry Jens. The patterns that bound them and upheld them were too polarizing to coexist. But their need for each other was so strong that when their relationship broke, they broke as well. The damage, however, extends beyond them, setting the stage for violence and death.

In this early novel, Sorensen presents readers with all the possibilities of the Mormon pattern meeting worldly patterns—an essential question for her generation and ours. But in the end, she admits that she can only see it ending in destruction. And, indeed, it often did—and often does. However, Virginia would explore this convergence twice more, in *The Evening and the Morning* and *Many*

---

16. Sorensen, *On This Star*, 92.
17. Sorensen, *On This Star*, 108.
18. Sorensen, *On This Star*, 146.
19. Sorensen, *On This Star*, 167.

Heavens, each time as a more mature person and writer. She would find different endings each time.

On This Star, probably Sorensen's most accessible novel, is full of rewards. It features Seenie, Sorensen's most poignant secondary character. It also showcases Sanpete County's local color to great effect. It poetically explores Mormon temple ceremonies and builds many meanings around the temple structure itself. Both readers who are still firmly in the LDS Church and those who have exited will feel themselves intimately understood and portrayed. In many ways, this novel is Virginia at her best.

The Neighbors (1947)

At the beginning of *The Neighbors*, a large family (and, interestingly, an ex-Mormon one) drives through a rugged Colorado valley high in the mountains. They are on their way to the sheep ranch John Kels, the father of the brood, recently bought. Before this journey, he had been a high school history teacher, but now he is bent on returning to the land-focused lifestyle he knew as a child, hoping that this will be a return to Eden—for both him and his family.

But, as they soon find out, Phineas Roe is bent on driving them out so that he can buy their land and own the entire valley. He starts by trying to hire away Ed, their sheepherder. Then he diverts a school-teaching job in the valley away from Ann, John's oldest daughter, and gives it to his own daughter, Cloie. He refuses to allow his own family to fraternize with the Kels family. As expected, Roe's effect on his own household is an onerous one, weighing down Roe's blind son, Brad; daughter-in-law, Alice; and grandchildren. "Words moved between them as through a sick black sea."[20]

John does not quite know what he has gotten into with the ranch. He relies completely on Ed for the sheepherding. He makes a fool of himself at an association meeting of local sheep ranchers, trying to introduce new co-operative ideas and receiving only thinly veiled mockery. He finds out that he has arrived in the middle of—and is now behind on—an important part of the sheep-ranching cycle, and that this cycle will dominate every aspect of his family's life

---

20. Virginia Sorensen, *The Neighbors* (New York: Reynal and Hitchcock, 1947), 291.

from now on. They only have their small ranch to work with, being hemmed in on all sides by Roe's holdings. No growth is possible, only maintenance.

Strangely, the story does not focus on the family's struggles to stay afloat; neither does it focus on how they try to integrate with the rest of the valley; neither does it build up the conflict between the Kels and the Roes. Bits and pieces of these plot threads pop up now and then, but never take a serious hold on the story. In fact, nothing seems to take a hold of the story. Halfway through the book, Marie Kels dies, but leaves only a few ripples in her wake. Fifty of the Kelses' sheep are killed in a lightning strike, and Call Kels and Cloie Roe fall into forbidden love—but suddenly the novel jumps ahead six months without pursuing the consequences. Rather than building a story, the prose—poetic, beautiful, insightful—presents slices of life: following one of the novel's many characters into their thoughts, their pasts, their conversations—then following another.

This lack of plot progression makes it seem as if this valley is indeed an Eden, but the Mormon version of Eden, where no sustained conflict, and therefore no growth, occurs. Things change, but the changes mean little. That is, until the last thirty pages of the book hit.

Roe has deployed another tactic to damage the Kels family, secretly diverting some of their water share onto his own land. After discovering it, John lies in wait for him one night, but Roe sends his blind son, Brad, to divert the water instead, and after a brief clash with John, Brad falls, hits his head, and dies instantly. Roe wants to prosecute John, but his daughter-in-law and Cloie threaten to ruin him. The emotional and financial monopoly Roe has held over his family disintegrates, and, with no one to rule, he finds himself without an identity. Paulie Kels, the mother of the family, steps in and presents a way for Roe to integrate with the family. The integration breaks the gridlock that Roe had asserted on the valley and his family, making room for the Kels family to grow financially and Roe to grow emotionally.

It is a sudden ending to a wandering novel, and its image of a first-born, best-beloved son dying seems to demand that readers interpret the novel scripturally; and if they do, it seems to turn the normal interpretation of Christ's redeeming death on its head.

Perhaps this is a story about what would happen if Adam returned to Eden from the lone and dreary world—not heroically, but still full of sin. What he finds there is not a wise God who had sent Adam forth for a wise purpose, but a domineering God who expelled him to keep Eden perfect. This God uses all his power to eject Adam again so that he can erect a final barrier between them. In the end, it is God's own machinations that kill his beloved son. It was the overwhelming weight of God's judgment, God's own relentless insistence that only perfection could enter his kingdom, that accidentally brought about the Atonement. He did not send his son in mercy, rather, he inadvertently made him into a sacrifice that brought down his kingdom and forced him to integrate with humanity.

The strange lack of story progression that slows the novel seems to bear this interpretation out. If nothing could progress in the Garden of Eden, nothing could progress in the story either.

The most interesting thing is that Paulie—the mother of the Kels clan, and therefore Eve in this allegorical reading—is the one who offers Roe his chance at the beginnings of salvation. Having been a somewhat secondary character the entire novel, she is quietly more religious than John; she is the practical ballast of the family, keeping them steady. For these qualities, John sometimes sees her as dull and backward. But she is the one who resolves the novel, by playing the role of Eve.

Mormon theology maintains that Eve should be honored for first stepping foot into the lone and dreary world, because it was only there that humans could progress. In *The Neighbors*, it seems that Paulie, as Eve, is once again the portal between worlds, but this time a portal for God to escape the weight of his own judgment—the strangulating stasis of Eden—and enter into growth alongside humanity. "Let him be saved," she says. "It will save us all."[21]

The Evening and the Morning (1949)

Mormons have a hard time approving of *The Evening and the Morning*. It is, after all, the story of a woman (Kate Alexander) who unrepentantly carries on a long-term affair in a small Mormon town—*and* she is presented sympathetically. This does not sit well

---

21. Sorensen, *The Neighbors*, 310.

with orthodox Mormons; it looks too much like (maybe even *exactly* like) an attempt at making wickedness appear as happiness.

Everything else about the novel seems almost scriptural: Its title, referencing the Genesis creation story; its language, like poetry spun out over hundreds of pages; its epic, yet intimate, feel; and the fact that just about every sentence can be read and re-read, each time revealing a new layer of meaning. It is the kind of novel that finds its way onto "desert island" book lists.

What makes this novel able to completely transcend its summary? It is like the biblical story of Hosea marrying the harlot Gomer, or the story of Abraham sacrificing Isaac: stories that push hard against the good and proper. But for what reason? Perhaps *The Evening and the Morning* gets its power from the fact that it seems to be—strangely enough—a conversion story.

How does a conversion story go? Someone encounters the truth and is overwhelmed by it. Its power is irresistible. The convert must embrace it. Sacrifice, joy, and agony follow.

Throughout Sorensen's work, that kind of conversion manifests itself when a woman falls in love with a man—in this case, when Kate falls in love with Peter. "With a man a woman really loves and desires, there is no pretense possible. She goes simply to him when he speaks to her."[22] "Shall I confess," Kate writes to Peter, "that because of you I have believed that life can be worth living even when it doesn't seem to be?"[23] The fact that both Kate and Peter are already in marriages has no bearing on this love, the same as when a person who is already involved with a religion is helpless but to embrace the truth. It does not matter how kind one's husband is or how supportive one's church. Love is love.

Of course, the convert is suddenly at odds with their community, just as Kate is suddenly at odds with her family and church. Early Mormonism developed a solution for its converts' sudden alienation by summoning them to Zion. But what happens when one is converted but must continue to live in one's community—when one cannot escape to Zion? This is Kate and Peter's plight. They must

---

22. Virginia Sorensen, *The Evening and the Morning* (New York: Harcourt, Brace and Co., 1949), 263.

23. Sorensen, *The Evening and the Morning*, 63.

keep quiet. They can only unite occasionally. The consequences of being discovered would be devastating. But it is all worth it, because they are each other's one connection to love. "What she has done for her lover [is] a separate thing hovering above the earth," Kate reflects, "as irreproachable as a rainbow and as fantastically capable ... of providing rich reward where it touches the earth."[24]

Is not that the way we tell conversion stories? If a convert is required to give up home, job, family, even life, it is all the more reason to honor their strength. Truth is worth any sacrifice. Sorensen believes that the same is true of love. Peter recounts with great pride how his father left his child and pregnant wife behind in Denmark to move to Zion, having faith that she would be converted and follow him.[25] How different is it that Kate leaves two children behind in the care of their aunts as a consequence of her love for Peter? Why should Peter's father be admired and Kate not? Why can't religious conversion and love be on the same footing? They are, after all, the same thing: a complete reconstruction of the heart—despite the destruction they cause.

But all this happened long ago. Kate's husband died, and his sister-in-law threatened to expose Kate's affair, forcing her to move away. Kate is now in her fifties, a grandmother, returning to her Utah home after many years to gather information for a government pension. While she is here, readers see the results of her love for Peter: a daughter (by Peter) worried about her "Jack-Mormon" husband, a granddaughter just crossing the threshold of adolescence, both of them as out of place as Kate was. During the course of the book, readers get to know them and their struggles intimately.

The information Kate is most keen on getting, however, is about Peter. His wife is dead, and the possibility of reunion with him has never been far from Kate's mind. Can it be as it once was? At the end of the novel, when Kate arrives at Peter's home, he dutifully offers to reconnect, but she hears in his words "the terrible burden of obligation."[26] The man she loved is gone. "How much of him had she created for herself, she wondered, in order to love him perfectly?"[27]

---

24. Sorensen, *The Evening and the Morning*, 263.
25. She does not.
26. Sorensen, *The Evening and the Morning*, 334.
27. Sorensen, *The Evening and the Morning*, 333.

Conversion is not about the religion. Love is not about the be-loved. In the end, they are about the act: of belief, of love—and that can only stem from oneself. "Each one making what order he could from his own chaos."[28] Travelling home, Kate stares out the train window into the night as her granddaughter sleeps on her lap, watching "herself, moving beside herself, out there alone."[29]

In this final scene, readers see Sorensen considering again the plight of the returning Mormon. In *On This Star*, Erik inadvertently wreaks havoc on his family and community when he returns to Templeton. In this novel readers see Kate as more self-possessed, less destructive, but still unable to reintegrate with the community. Five years later, Sorensen would explore one more Mormon's return in *Many Heavens*.

The Evening and the Morning is rich with Mormon culture, sat-urated with Utah color, riddled with family tensions, but the story sublimates them all into something utterly more. "In the space available to me it is impossible to convey the whole richness of this novel," Dale Morgan wrote in a review of the book.[30] Indeed, to read *The Evening and the Morning* is to wonder how such a perfect novel was ever written ... and to wonder how it was ever forgotten.

The Proper Gods (1951)

The Proper Gods is the most unusual of Virginia Sorensen's novels; it is also one of her least read works. However, it marks the most important turning point in her authorial vision, affecting every book that came afterward. As she said, the book "had a bearing on every-thing I have done since, even upon the 'Mormon' writing."[31]

Nothing about *The Proper Gods* feels anything like what Sorensen had published before. It takes place in a Yaqui village in Mexico. It has a male protagonist. It has no Mormons in it. It has barely a whiff of Sorensen's gentle feminism. And those are just its cosmetic elements. The novel reads as if Sorensen had written it in a language

---

28. Sorensen, *The Evening and the Morning*, 341.

29. Sorensen, *The Evening and the Morning*, 341.

30. Dale L. Morgan, "Fruits of Rebellion," *Saturday Review*, Apr. 23, 1949, 13.

31. Virginia Sorensen, "Is It True?—The Novelist and His Materials," *Western Humanities Review* 7, no. 4 (Autumn 1953): 286.

she had learned by rote, as if she were trying to manage a complicated piece of machinery by memorizing the operating manual.

This is almost literally the case. In Sorensen's previous novels she drew from decades of experience in Mormonism, often integrating her own memories and family stories into the narrative. With *The Proper Gods* she had to start from square one.

The book began as a side-interest Sorensen developed as she researched in Sonora, Mexico, a novel she was writing about Mormon maverick Sam Brannan. As she told a conference of University of Utah writers, she became acquainted with the Yaqui, and "in the Yaqui villages, I had the privilege of going to the Day of Dead Fiestas." In her files one finds snapshots of Sorensen with an elderly Yaqui woman. "Those studies," she said, "were among the happiest of my life."[32] After her in-person experiences with the Yaqui, Sorensen spent the next few years immersing herself in their history and anthropological studies about them.

What she came out with was the story of Adan, a young Yaqui man recently discharged from the US army and traveling to Potam, Mexico, his ancestral village. This seems a familiar beginning, as Sorensen's characters are often returning to their homelands, but there is a twist. Adan grew up in exile in Pascua, an Arizona village; his family relocated to Potam while he was away in the army. Instead of returning to the community he inhabited in his youth where he could interact intuitively, he enters a culture mostly unknown to him. It is a truth he learns quickly enough when he talks to a girl and is immediately struck by a nearby man. In Potam, boys do not talk to girls to whom they are not related—and they certainly do not talk to the fiancé of the captain of the village guard. The incident requires that Adan go to a "junta" where his crime will be judged and punished. And life only gets more complicated from there. It is not so much that Adan is a round peg trying to fit into a square hole; it is more that he is a foreign object tossed deep inside an intricate, brutal machine.

As Adan struggles to understand the labyrinthine workings of Potam culture, so does the reader. Huge swaths of text are dedicated to describing daily patterns, gender expectations, legalities, history,

---

32. Sorensen, "Is It True?," 287.

rituals, holidays. As Sorensen admitted, "Whenever you write about a 'peculiar people' you will find yourself under the necessity of holding up the action of your stories in a way most frowned-upon by the technicians, while you explain how your characters feel about heaven and hell, and why."[33] As Western readers move further into the novel, they likely find Potam's culture restrictive to the point of suffocation. Adan certainly does. After a lecture from his grandfather, who is a kind of village holy man, "Adan thanked him as if for a good lesson. But it was like another great loop in a net which surrounded a man."[34]

Potam's rigid culture stands in contrast to that of the Mexicans who live nearby. As a Mexican army captain drives Adan to Potam, he encourages him to take up modern farming practices and bring extra money into the village. Adan finds staunch resistance to such an idea. When he sells some cane at the Mexican border (a forbidden transaction), his grandfather insists that he use his earnings to buy an image for the church altar.

That is the basic tension of the narrative: the highly ritualized, communitarian culture of the Yaqui in contrast with the more capitalistic, individualistic culture of the Mexicans. The pressure of Potam's culture turns out to be too much for Adan's younger sister, Juana, who runs away with Teo, one of Adan's Mexican acquaintances. As she tells him, "I felt after that, Adan, that I was the stone in Potam. He [Grandfather] meant it to be like that with me, and it was. But one thing he did not understand, that I was not like that stone when I was with Teo—I was alive then."[35]

Despite his difficulty with the culture, Adan puts a lot of work into making himself fit in so that he can marry a local girl with whom he has fallen in love. He joins a group of men, called the *chapayekas*, who are tasked with preparing the village for its largest festival. During this time, he starts to see value beneath the numerous rituals. "If one carried these squashes in a procession instead of heaped together on Molonoko's old wagon," Adan thinks one day, "would they not become something else in the mind, something

---

33. Sorensen, "Is It True?," 290.

34. Virginia Sorensen, *The Proper Gods* (New York: Harcourt, Brace, and Co., 1951), 182.

35. Sorensen, *Proper Gods*, 154.

better than squashes?"[36] "It occurred to him for the first time what an amazing number of things might go through a man's head as he knelt before an altar in his house."[37]

The burdens of life, however, weigh heavily on his family—their crops withering in the sun while he is out performing his numerous ceremonial duties. Then his baby niece falls ill, invoking the specter of the village's high infant mortality rate. One night, during a holy time when no one is allowed to work, Adan sneaks out to water his crops. The next day he is captured by a fellow *chapayeka* and put in the village stocks where he suffers physically and emotionally for days as the holy week ceremonies continue around him. The humiliation cements his plan to leave the village as his sister Juana did—and as his older sister and brother-in-law are planning to do.

When he is finally released, it seems that everyone in the village has forgiven, and even forgotten, his crime. The way seems open for him to become an integrated part of the community. Indeed, the village marshals its resources to help Adan afford his expensive marriage rituals. The onerous burden of this ritualized culture brings with it a tightly knit, supportive community. "What a different thing from the Mexican way of doing, or the Americano way, each for himself. A Yaqui belonged not only to his own people but to all those who were obligated to him as he to them, so the great web of kinship, blood and ceremonial together, spread out over all the villages."[38]

Toward the end of the book, Adan's grandfather, who has represented and enforced traditional Yaqui culture in Adan's family, dies, and Adan finds himself in charge of the mourning and burial rituals. "He began to speak, and the ritual flowed from him like rain from the sky. He had never spoken like this in his life, even the old ritual with passion and gratitude. For he felt it deeply, every word. It was not a ritual at all, not automatic any longer. He heard it word by word as he spoke it. He even understood now what it was to be one who had sinned and been forgiven."[39]

In the end, Adan decides that he will stay in Potam and invest himself in traditional Yaqui culture. How does the story treat this

36. Sorensen, *Proper Gods*, 180.
37. Sorensen, *Proper Gods*, 115.
38. Sorensen, *Proper Gods*, 177.
39. Sorensen, *Proper Gods*, 305.

climax? Looking back, it is surprising to see that the story was not constructed to convince us that Adan's decision was correct. Rather it puts us in a position where we are able to feel the full *weight* of Adan's decision. That weight is significant. Potam is still poverty-stricken. Its infant mortality rate is still high. None of the problems disappear because Adan makes his commitment. "There is always a ceremony to lose a job for, but not always a job to lose."[40]

On the other hand, the problems that plague the Mexican culture surrounding Potam also remain. Yes, Juana has found an essential freedom she could not have in Potam. Adan's sister will likely be able to find medicine to cure her child. But with that freedom comes a significant diminishment of community support and an impoverishment of life narrative. "The world is like a great desert, with millions of tiny trails abandoned while you passed."[41]

It is quite an experience to come out the other side of *The Proper Gods*. Every page has been work; every paragraph, and sometimes every sentence, has presented a new piece of an alien matrix, one that seems to have almost no referent in a Western world view. What do readers do inside a culture of such unique shape and function?

It seems that Sorensen wrote this novel as a way of releasing herself and her readers from our own point of view—from the invisible programming we judge life by. The way she did it was to baptize readers by immersion into this very un-Western culture at enough length and in enough detail that they could finally intuit two essential things: the Yaqui culture's undeniable validity and the reader's complete lack of authority to judge it.

If readers can go the entire distance with *The Proper Gods*, being forced to see everything with beginner's eyes, they realize that the purpose of the book is not to help them understand the Yaqui culture.[42] Rather, they are to feel what it is like to see the world anew. "It is not new insights that are important in writing," Sorensen said, "but new seeing."[43]

---

40. Sorensen, *Proper Gods*, 292.

41. Sorensen, *Proper Gods*, 289.

42. However, Sorensen insisted on getting the cultural elements as correct as she possibly could, running drafts past Edward and Rosamond Spicer, anthropologists who had close connections to the Yaqui.

43. Sorensen, "Is It True?," 288.

Researching and writing *The Proper Gods* seems to have been a kind of baptism for Sorensen herself, deeply affecting the rest of her novels. It marks the first time one of her characters returns to their community and integrates with it.[44] Characters in previous novels return, but either find tragedy (*On This Star*) or disappointment (*The Evening and the Morning*). These characters (and probably Sorensen herself) are constantly judging the culture from which they came. *The Proper Gods* taught Sorensen how to feel a culture's full credence and find ways of creating within its confines. She brought that lesson with her into her first post-*Proper Gods* Mormon novel, *Many Heavens*, which features a returning character who not only integrates with the community, but integrates his outside experiences and world views with even its fundamentalist aspects. A few years later, Sorensen took matters a step farther when she published *Kingdom Come*, a novel about nineteenth-century Danes who join the LDS Church, which some reviewers commented could have been published by the church itself.

Interestingly, Sorensen was far out of the LDS Church by the time *The Proper Gods* was published, and she would eventually join the Anglican Church when she married Alec Waugh. But her experience with *The Proper Gods* seemed to help her develop a constructive peace with her Mormon roots and with the many other cultures she would encounter throughout her globe-trotting life.

Many Heavens (1954)

Many Heavens is Sorensen's most surprising book for one reason: she somehow made polygamy seem palatable, even sweet, to a general American audience—in the middle of the 1950s!

The story rests on a simple premise: there is, indeed, a one-and-only for each of us. One of Sorensen's great gifts is to help the reader remember what it is like to be absolutely in love, and soon she has readers emotionally convinced that there really is a joyful resonance that can only exist between two specific people. That resonance expresses itself both emotionally and physically.

For example, one female character, Dell, gets kissed by a particular boy and "for the first time in her life she knew what kissing was

---

44. Whether that integration is a good thing or not seems left up to the reader.

really like. After that, knowing what she knew, she made chances whenever she could. She never even thought about it being wrong, because it wasn't; it was so right she had never known anything so good in all her life. ... and afterward Dell could scarcely walk sometimes, for happiness. It was as if she had no legs at all but a kind of tremulous spirit moving over the earth."[45]

Even if the reader's head is not convinced of the one-and-only, soon Sorensen's luminous prose and tender descriptions convince the reader's heart.

This is where the problems begin. Because the protagonist, Zina, falls in one-and-only love with a married man, Niels. He grew up in the small Mormon valley (patterned after Cache Valley), went on a mission to Europe, stayed to get a medical degree, and returned to marry one of the most accomplished, athletic, and beautiful girls in the valley, Mette. Almost immediately after their wedding (in a church, rather than in a temple), a train wreck cripples Mette. The couple spends a few years back East going from doctor to doctor, but eventually returns to the valley where Niels sets up his practice.

Zina is brought in to be Mette's caretaker, and they soon come to love and respect one another. Along the way, Zina's parochial eyes are opened by the worldly and scientific texts Niels reads aloud to Mette while Zina is there. "Together they pulled the blind tough skin of accostumedness from my eyes. ... Niels brought the world to the valley and Mette somehow fitted it in."[46] A hunger for knowledge starts to awaken inside Zina, along with a hunger for Niels. And Niels starts falling in love with Zina—emotionally, intellectually, and physically.

Watching their romance unfold is one of the great pleasures of *Many Heavens*, Sorensen keeping their fierce attraction in aching tension with their responsibilities. Indeed, a single line looms over them, "One woman never in this world walked to happiness over the body of another."[47] Though Sorensen takes readers deeply into the flourishing intimacy between Zina and Niels, she never lets them forget that Mette's heart is of equal value. As Zina puts it, "It was

---

45. Virginia Sorensen, *Many Heavens* (New York: Harcourt, Brace and Co., 1954), 134.
46. Sorensen, *Many Heavens*, 49.
47. Sorensen, *Many Heavens*, 149.

familiar enough later, that awful confusion, the two emotions thrusting from opposite sides so that I was helpless between them."[48]

Yes, it is one of the oldest stories there is: the love triangle. But with a twist this time, because the action takes place only a few years after the 1890 Woodruff Manifesto had renounced polygamy, which caused a stir in the valley, even driving its beloved, long-time, polygamous bishop (Mette's father) to Canada to live plural marriage away from prying eyes. This new romance could have been easily resolved only a few years earlier, with Niels taking Zina as a plural wife. But would it have really been resolved? A marriage would have happened; but what about the hearts involved?

Zina decides to go get a nursing degree in Salt Lake City, much to Mette's relief—she can see what is happening between Niels and Zina. But they cannot keep apart. So, toward the end of the book, Zina decides she is going to move to the East after her graduation, scholarship in hand, to earn her own medical degree.

This time, Mette stops her and offers her a place in the family.

It is a strange scene to modern sensibilities. Mette recounts how her father's first wife, Dinah, could not bear children but wanted them desperately. So, she brought in a newly immigrated Danish girl, Margrethe, to keep house and then, one day, spruced her up and presented her to her husband. It was something that happened from time to time during that period, though Mette admits, "they didn't all turn out so well."[49]

Though the children who filled the house after that did not come from Dinah, "she knew there was a special room in Father's heart where she belonged."[50]

"'Niels loves you very much,' [Mette] said, and if she winced I didn't see it. 'I've known it for a long time. But I've known still longer that he loves me. For different things, in different ways. Why should all of us go on suffering so much?'"[51]

At this point readers may feel they have missed the most interesting part of the story: Mette's journey. They have been so involved

48. Sorensen, *Many Heavens*, 103.
49. Sorensen, *Many Heavens*, 347.
50. Sorensen, *Many Heavens*, 347.
51. Sorensen, *Many Heavens*, 346.

in the romance between Zina and Niels that they have not walked with Mette through what was doubtless the weightiest decision of her life. Further, how did Niels, being in love with Zina as well, convince Mette's heart of his love? Would readers have balked at another hundred pages to watch this story unfold? Not if Virginia Sorensen were writing it.

At the end of the novel, the one-and-only still stands unscathed, but love has been diversified—given more rooms. More heavens.

Sorensen's powers are on full display in this novel: the poetic language, the emotional insight, the ethnographic eye, the gripping story. It is also the novel where Sorensen's returning Mormon character finally succeeds. Like Erik Eriksen and Kate Alexander before him, Niels goes on his hero's journey into the "capitals of culture" and returns. But instead of finding death or rejection, he integrates his new self with the people he sprang from, even to the point of taking on one of their most peculiar practices and transforming it into a relationship where the heart, rather than the institution, is most important.

Kingdom Come (1960)

Kingdom Come was Virginia's last Mormon novel, but it was not meant to be. She actually wrote it as the first book in a planned trilogy, but the second and third books never came to pass. There are any number of reasons why a person might not finish writing a trilogy,[52] but, in this case, lack of time was not one of them. After releasing *Kingdom Come*, Virginia still had another thirty-one years of life in front of her, eighteen of which saw her actively publishing. So why did the next two novels never arrive? Possibly because Sorensen made little money from *Kingdom Come* and preferred to turn her efforts toward the more lucrative children's book market.[53] On the other hand, perhaps she stopped at the first book because it sufficiently sounded the last essential note her collection of Mormon novels needed to resonate fully with each other.

---

52. Especially since the trilogy would probably have totaled about 1,500 pages.

53. Which she did. She released her children's novels *Lotte's Locket, Around the Corner*, and *Friends of the Road* after *Kingdom Come*. She only released one other novel for adults, *The Man with the Key*. But none of these were commercial or critical successes.

The thing that strikes most readers about *Kingdom Come* (besides its heft—weighing in at nearly 500 pages) is how different it is from Virginia's other Mormon novels. It takes place in Denmark during the mid-1800s. Mormonism is not even mentioned until 150 pages in. The book follows the stories of Danish converts to Mormonism in such a way that readers may wonder if the church's own publisher, Deseret Book, would have been willing to publish it. Where are the complexities of faith and doubt? Why is the book filled to the brim with believers? Why is the entire narrative proceeding in an orthodox direction?

The story begins deep in Danish culture, far out in Jutland—a place whose inhabitants think of going to Copenhagen as a once-in-a-lifetime endeavor. There, readers meet Hanne Dalsgaard, the only daughter of a well-to-do couple and belle of the village. In the servants' house lives Svend Madsen, a teenage orphan who wandered through the countryside until he was given a job farming the Dalsgaard estate. And, this being a Virginia Sorensen novel, Hanne and Svend are drawn together, soon falling in love. Hanne's parents are not keen on the match. After a lavish christening party, Hanne stays out late with Svend—and the whole village knows about it. Her parents immediately pack her off to Copenhagen; Svend is fired and joins the army.

While serving, Svend meets Simon Peter, who has what the soldiers call "preaching sickness." Despite Simon Peter's frequent sermons, he and Svend become friends. Their outfit returns to Copenhagen in glory after winning an important battle where Svend meets Simon Peter's religious community—Baptists. Then Simon Peter hears that missionaries from a new American religion are in town. When they meet these missionaries, Apostle Snow (based on Erastus Snow, who served a mission in Denmark around the time the story takes place) connects Svend with his long-lost brother—a reunion Svend has desired his whole life.

Soon, both Svend and Simon Peter become converted. Not only that, they become missionaries. Not only that, Svend goes back to the Dalsgaard estate and preaches the Mormon gospel to the families with whom he used to work—with great success. Then he departs for a proselytizing mission to Norway. Hanne considers

Svend lost to her and drifts into an engagement with a man from Copenhagen, though it has none of the spark she experienced when she was with Svend.

Then Svend returns, and the couple's passion reignites. He proclaims his unending love to Hanne, and she gives herself to him as well. He heads back home where he writes her a letter promising to return from his mission to Norway and marry her. But the letter is intercepted by the local pastor, and Hanne's mother intercepts Svend's other letters. Hanne is left thinking Svend has abandoned her; meanwhile, Svend is bewildered by her lack of response.

Through hook and crook, Hanne retrieves Svend's original letter and realizes what has happened. Within a day she leaves her mother and father and travels to Copenhagen where she lives with a community of Mormons.[54] By the end of the novel, Hanne and Svend are reunited, sailing with the other Danish converts toward England where they will depart for America.

One's head almost spins to see how orthodox the trajectory of *Kingdom Come*'s story is. Nothing in Virginia's previous novels would lead readers to anticipate it. What in the world happened?

The most likely answer is that *Kingdom Come* is the first act of the story Sorensen was planning. In traditional story structures the first act sets up the story's characters and sends them on an adventure, and the next two acts are about that adventure—where things get messy. Taking this approach, the second book might be about Hanne and Svend's journey across the ocean, and then across America to reach Utah. The third book might be about the lives they build in Utah. These next two novels would be where the Virginia we know would start to emerge as she sends her characters through the terrible hardships of their cross-continental journey, and then into the complexities of being a Latter-day Saint in early Utah.

Indeed, we see the seeds of those next two acts being planted in *Kingdom Come*. Svend receives a blessing from Apostle Snow promising him "wives." While Svend languishes in a Norwegian jail, he starts to become attracted to the jailer's daughter. The missionaries

---

54. Sorensen effectively shows how devastating Hanne's sudden departure is to her parents, acknowledging the real family trauma that Mormon conversion and emigration could cause.

even have an oblique conversation about rumors of plural marriage. Rather than being offended by it, they speak of it as a great blessing they may someday become worthy of.

Plural marriage would be a huge difficulty in this case because, as with most of Virginia's female characters, Hanne is irrevocably in love with one man.[55] But, as with most of Virginia's male characters, Svend is in love with Mormonism. We see parallels between Hanne and Svend and Mercy and Simon (in *A Little Lower Than the Angels*), especially since, like Mercy, Hanne follows the Mormons because she loves Svend, not because she is converted. Indeed, she has not even been baptized when they depart on the ship for England.[56]

We could take another approach too. Virginia was in love with Denmark, with her ancestors, and with a good story. The narrative she was planning had all three. She spent months researching for *Kingdom Come* in Demark, and, as pointed out in *The Proper Gods* section, Sorensen had developed the capacity to love a culture on its own terms by then. Perhaps she was applying that love to the story of the Danish Saints.[57]

In either case, we encounter a truly epic story stretching out in front of us, being spun by an experienced author who had everything she needed to bring it off in style. It is possible that if Sorensen had brought the whole project to fruition, we might have the long-sought-after Great Mormon Novel in our hands by now.

But what *do* we have in *Kingdom Come*? In a way, we finally have the first act for every previous Mormon novel Virginia had written. Her other novels were very much in the vein of the second and third acts: filled with messy characters whose thrilling youthful beginnings

---

55. As the ship pulls away from shore, Hanne looks at the people standing on the dock. "They must be satisfied to exist where they stood, like trees. But if a great wind blows at you and it is Svend, what could you do? Otherwise you would die at the root" (496).

56. Virginia actually revealed part of Hanne's storyline for the future books in a letter to Virginia Eddings. "Svend went back on a mission and brought home a Norwegian girl he converted, daughter of the jailer, you recall. Hanne couldn't stomach another wife and was a convert on his account anyhow—so she inherited Johannedal ... and went back [to Denmark] to play the organ." Quoted in William Mulder, "History, Memory, and Imagination in Virginia Eggertsen Sorensen's *Kingdom Come*," *Dialogue: A Journal of Mormon Thought* 35, no. 1 (Spring 2002): 98.

57. There is a third approach as well, which Virginia contemplated: focusing each book on a succeeding generation of the family.

had run into diverse paths, becoming ever more individual, complicated, and intimate. These novels certainly stand on their own, but *Kingdom Come* can give them even more weight as it reminds readers of the compelling vision these characters, this religion, and this culture sprang from. People were in fact willing to sacrifice all they had to follow this new gospel into a strange land. They really did build a kingdom in the desert. Without that story at the foundation of Sorensen's novels (either haunting them or supporting them), they cannot be fully understood or valued. *Kingdom Come* is the first movement in the symphony Sorensen had been building, book by book, for eighteen years.

Where Nothing Is Long Ago: Memories of a Mormon Childhood (1963)

In Sorensen's children's novels, her deep connection to childhood is on full display, but her childhood itself shows up almost not at all. This is not surprising since her children's novels are set in just about every place except Utah (with the exception of *The House Next Door*, but it takes place sixteen years before Sorensen's birth and in urban Salt Lake City). But in *Where Nothing Is Long Ago: Memories of a Mormon Childhood*, readers finally get a sumptuous (and slightly fictionalized) banquet of her time growing up in Manti, Utah.

"I see now what a paradise of space we had to live in," Sorensen wrote to her childhood friend Carol Reid Holt, and the ten short stories that comprise *Where Nothing Is Long Ago* present that paradise luminously. Two of the stories were originally published in the *New Yorker*, but readers would never be able to tell which ones; all of them show Sorensen at the height of her authorial powers.

Like Ray Bradbury's *Dandelion Wine*, the stories evoke both the magic and the hauntedness of being a child: that time in life when the world can flip from enchantment to terror in a moment—when the boundaries between one's self and the world are thin, sometimes disappearing altogether.

Indeed, appearance and disappearance tie these stories together. No one is immune to the possibility of being erased—or suddenly revealed.

In "The Darling Lady" Sorensen's young self realizes that a woman she has been buying groceries from had disappeared into the confines of her tiny, two-room shop decades earlier when her polygamous marriage was no longer recognized and her place in the community vanished. For years, she inhabited a different world, a different time flow. "How slowly she had always moved," Sorensen writes. "She must have had a terrible lot of time."[58]

A similar disappearance occurs in the title story when, in a fit of rage, Brother Tolsen accidentally kills a man who was diverting Tolsen's water, one of the most serious crimes in pioneering Utah when water was more precious than gold. The man not only disappears from life "knocked headlong 'through the veil' with a shovel,"[59] he disappears from the moral fabric of the community, remembered only as a water thief, all sympathy going to Brother Tolsen. "Is it not true that he who steals water is stealing life itself?"[60] Tolsen's lawyer argues. Soon, the dead man's wife disappears into "that vast place … Great Salt Lake City."[61]

The strangest disappearance and revelation takes place in "The Ghost," the story of the summer a Black family visits Manti for a few months. The father of the family comes to church, having been converted by one of the local men on a mission to the South, and his dark skin stands in marked contrast to the largely Danish-descended congregation. The only person who seems happy to see him is the music conductor when he hears the man's beautiful voice booming through the chapel during sacrament meeting hymns. (The man never gets a name; the narrator simply calls him "the Negro.")

The family stays in a tent up the canyon for a few months, and soon the Halloween party at church rolls around. Someone shows up wearing a full-length ghost costume that completely obscures his body and face. The ghost becomes the center of attention as he dances with every female he can rustle up. The organizers soon become convinced that the ghost is "the Negro" and that he must be removed from the party as quickly as possible. But they are Mormons, so they find a nice way to do it. They announce the winners of the costume contest, giving first prize to the ghost, insisting that

---

58. Virginia Sorensen, *Where Nothing Is Long Ago: Memories of a Mormon Childhood* (New York: Harcourt, Brace, and World, Inc., 1963), 27.

59. Sorensen, *Where Nothing Is Long Ago*, 10.

60. Sorensen, *Where Nothing Is Long Ago*, 14.

61. Sorensen, *Where Nothing Is Long Ago*, 13.

he remove his costume to receive his prize. The sheet comes off to reveal, instead, a Danish-white member of the local congregation.

The most disconcerting disappearance occurs in "The Face." Pubescent Virginia is climbing out of the bathtub and reaching for a towel one night when she notices a face staring down at her from the top of the unobscured portion of the bathroom window. Her parents run out to see if they can catch the lurker, and they notify the sheriff who comes over to look for tracks. He says that no strangers are in town right now, so the peeping Tom must have been a local.

As Virginia walks to the store the next day, she scans every person she passes to see if theirs matches the face she saw in the window. When her mother's friend comes over to do some canning, Virginia catches a look from her. "Suddenly I felt my clothes fall away in her mind. She *knew*. She was thinking how I had looked when the stranger stared into the window."[62] Then, when one of her brother's friends comes by, she sees him blush and look down. At the end of the story, the telephone rings and rings, every call coming from a concerned neighbor, every call erasing Virginia and replacing her with a story, an image, that someone else had thrust upon her.

Interestingly, *Where Nothing Is Long Ago* was not Sorensen's original choice for the collection's title; she wanted to call it *First Loves*, a direct reference to the story about ... her childhood cat (called "First Love"). Why would this story stand out in her mind as being most representative of the collection, especially when the story has no Mormon content? We might find an answer in a speech Sorensen gave at the University of Utah Writers Conference in 1953, where she probably startled everyone by stating, "I am not interested in Mormonism particularly. Not *particularly*."[63] If we dig deeply into her novels, we see that, indeed, it is not Mormonism she is *particularly* interested in, it only provides the structure inside of which Sorensen explores her true subject: love. "First Love" is not just about a cat, it is about the beautiful and heartbreaking ways love manifests itself—all of them playing out in the small, intimate space between a child and her pet.

---

62. Sorensen, *Where Nothing Is Long Ago*, 153.
63. Sorensen, "Is It True?," 287.

The most revealing story may be "The Apostate," which gives readers a map of how Sorensen became a writer. It starts with her young self, curled up in a small storage area beneath the stairs of her house that she enters through a miniature door. The room has a window that gives her a secret view of the people passing the house. "How many hours I spent in its light I cannot calculate, reading, writing verses, making secrets."[64] She shares that closet with the artifacts of her family's past, such as a trunk full of her grandfather's belongings including a watch that she winds up "and for days afterward I could hear it ticking fearsomely away in the trunk ... I never wound it again. The trunk seemed to me the very symbol of the grave."[65]

Then the narrative shifts to a dramatic religion class, where the teacher declaims the story of Joseph Smith's martyrdom in 1844 at the hands of "apostates." "Why should I not thrill to every tale?" she asks. "I was a Saint myself, baptized in the White Temple up on Temple Hill."[66]

Young Virginia finds out that her own grandmother is an apostate by her own admission, and it shatters her. The story spends its last pages with Virginia as she tends to her dying grandmother, reading the notes in her scriptures and other books, talking with her, hearing her difficult life story. She is very surprised when her grandmother insists on being buried in her sacred temple robes. "You don't believe in all that, Mother," says Virginia's mother. "You've said so ever since I can remember. So *why*—"

"I made a promise," her grandmother replies. "And when I make a promise, I keep it!"[67]

These three elements—the concentrated imagination of childhood, the potent stories of Mormonism, and the complexity of Virginia's ancestors—form the trinity of Sorensen's distinctive vision, combining and recombining to reveal her deep insights into love, relationships, and the human soul.

The Man with the Key (1974)

The Man with the Key is Sorensen's most contemporary book.

---

64. Sorensen, *Where Nothing Is Long Ago*, 42.
65. Sorensen, *Where Nothing Is Long Ago*, 42.
66. Sorensen, *Where Nothing Is Long Ago*, 47.
67. Sorensen, *Where Nothing Is Long Ago*, 56.

In it, a Danish woman, married to a Virginia college professor for twenty-five years, suddenly finds herself a widow, and—a few weeks after her bereavement—having an affair with a Black man half her age (she is forty-eight, he twenty-four).

Vesta, the protagonist, bumps up against many of the issues that have come into such stark relief since the rise of the Black Lives Matter movement: white privilege, affirmative action, racist language, microaggression, cultural appropriation, and allyship. The fact that all of this shows up in a 1974 novel is a testament that it has all indeed been around for longer than popular culture has been talking about it. Here we see Sorensen tentatively exploring it.

Vesta is an educated woman, teaching classes at a private university. Jimmie, her lover, is a custodian there. When he tries to explain his ideas in writing, Vesta recognizes his intelligence but cannot help but try to standardize his spelling and "complex" (his word) his thought.

The economic disparity between them becomes more and more apparent, as Vesta finds herself funding Jimmie's gas money, a vacation they take together, and then a business venture.

The damage the affair wreaks is greater on Jimmie than on Vesta. He slowly becomes estranged from his wife and children, while Vesta's son actually seems delighted with her affair—having grown up with Jimmie and being progressively minded.

In the end, Vesta has to leave the school, going to live for a while with her son and his fiancée, while Jimmie loses his job and any semblance of family stability.

The most poignant encounters Vesta has are with Christy, a Black student who takes one of Vesta's painting courses. Vesta signs on as a faculty advisor for a Black student club Christy is trying to start. The club application sets off alarms in the administration, however, where they worry that it is part of an effort to get the Black Power movement a foothold in academia, and eventually undermine the school itself. They find a way to reject the club's application and neuter its plans for Black Week at the school.

So Christy organizes the Black community and church to hold Black Week activities. But, after a bomb threat against a campus building, the school's student body and faculty are forbidden to attend. Vesta goes anyway. The events soon turn into the occupation of a campus building and a real bomb, all of it apparently carried out by Blacks. In other words, all the administration's worries come to pass.

Then Christy's group reveals the affair between Vesta and Jimmie, vandalizing her car in the process. They even plan, Vesta hears through a longtime Black housekeeper, to disfigure her with acid. Jimmie whisks her to a bus station to get her out of town.

Vesta is baffled by Christy's treatment of her; after all, Vesta had stuck her neck out for her a few times. But she had had a brief taste of Christy's fire during their last conversation. "The thing is, see, you could never know how it is. You've never had to take nobody's crap. The Vests, lady in the big house, you're the one I've hated my whole goddamned life. You come in here and smile at me and say, 'paint what you want to—paint *how you feel.*'"

"Now I was getting it out of her, from another place," Vesta thinks. Christy goes on, "Good God, what I want to paint couldn't hang on any wall in this place, do you know that? It'd be you and your committee running up the roads in your caps and gowns with red-hot pokers up every ass."[68]

The novel is written in first person, Vesta looking back on this year of her life. The reason for using first person is usually to give the reminiscing character an opportunity to add insight and wisdom that she did not have at the time—drawing out the *meaning* of the events. But Sorensen takes almost no advantage of this, leaving the events in their raw form. Indeed, Sorensen the author seems to have little to offer except these events—regarding them with as much confusion as her readers do.

Conclusion

As Sorensen wrote in 1953, "Much of the [Mormon] work of the years just past, especially fiction, has had this overtenderness on one hand, or has been overembittered on the other, much as the Mormon-Gentile feeling was for so many years. It seemed for a long time necessary to take sides."[69] But Sorensen's work escaped "taking sides" because she believed that "a novel is seldom an explanation,

---

68. Virginia Sorensen, *The Man with the Key* (New York: Harcourt, Brace, Jovanovich, 1974), 263.

69. Sorensen, "Is It True?," 284.

but rather an exploration."[70] But exploration was not an end in itself: she also believed that people "live deeply and healthfully and well only when their lives have meaning."[71] These two commitments, to exploration and to meaning, propelled and balanced her novels. She believed in "The necessity for creating freely, certainly, but something more, the responsibility of preserving some web of significance that men can live by."[72] She seemed to weave this web of significance best in her Mormon novels. Perhaps because it was in that context that the "sides" were strongest, where she had to work hardest to navigate their twin pulls.

---

70. Sorensen, "Is It True?," 291.
71. Sorensen, "Is It True?," 289.
72. Sorensen, "Is It True?," 289.

CHAPTER TEN

HER CHILDREN'S NOVELS

If one were to survey librarians across America, asking who Virginia Sorensen is, most would likely remember her as a children's author. Only librarians from the Intermountain West might remember her novels for adults. This is likely the correct order of things. Virginia did, after all, win the 1957 Newbery Medal for *Miracles on Maple Hill*,[1] and once a writer has a Newbery, she is immortal. Another of Virginia's children's novels, *Plain Girl*, won a Child Study Award. Virginia herself admitted that her children's books were the ones that provided her with the most consistent stream of income and fan mail. "Only children—and this *is* truly a difference—respond with such an outpouring of gratitude and appreciation that a writer for them feels he will never bother to write for adults again," she wrote in 1966.[2]

Virginia's children's novels are, in many respects, utterly different from her adult novels. Mormonism shows up in only one of her children's novels, and it does so as an alien culture. Rather, she writes about people living in a variety of places and cultures: farmers in Alabama, maple extractors in Pennsylvania, diplomats' children in Morocco, displaced Appalachians, and the Amish, to name a few.

It seems as though she had two separate careers, one in children's novels and one in adult novels, neither informing the other. This separation has continued into the present day. Two of Virginia's children's novels are still in print, while only three of her adult novels are available

---

1. She is the only Mormon to win a Newbery Medal, though others have won Newbery honors.
2. Virginia Sorensen, "Childhood Is a Strange Book," lecture in Salt Lake City, June 20, 1966, Virginia Sorensen Papers, MSS 1686, box 2, fd. 3, L. Tom Perry Special Collections, Harold B. Lee Library, Brigham Young University, Provo, Utah.

as ebooks. Meanwhile, many scholarly papers have been written about her adult novels, but almost none about her children's novels.[3] Why do Virginia's children's novels seem to be their own beast?

It is possible that this split started while she was living in Sonora, Mexico, researching for a novel about Sam Brannan. Brannan was called by Brigham Young to take a group of Mormons on a ship around the tip of South America to land in San Francisco. Once there, however, Brannan broke from Mormonism to become California's first gold-rush millionaire. He was also a book publisher and the first of a long line of ethically questionable real estate speculators. He spent much of his life in Sonora before dying in penury.

While Virginia was researching Brannan's life in Sonora, she came into contact with the Yaqui Indians who wrested her attention away from Brannan. She spent a few months becoming an amateur cultural anthropologist, living with and learning from the Yaqui, all the while taking meticulous notes. She did end up writing a novel about Brannan, but it was rejected by her publisher. However, her experience with the Yaqui was so compelling that she wrote a novel set in their culture as well. And this one did get published. Admittedly, it is probably the most difficult read of her novels (as Oliver LaFarge, author of *Laughing Boy*, wrote to her, "I have a feeling that you never did quite surmount your ethnological information"[4]), but it marked a turning point in her career. Until now, she had written novels from inside her own culture; this was the first time she tried to make her way into another culture deeply enough to find a story there.

That experience prepared Virginia for the next twenty years of her writing career as she applied the observational and empathetic tools she had refined among the Yaqui. As the wife of a college professor, she moved from school to school across the country, each move landing her in a new culture where she opened her eyes wide and dived into researching the place and its culture.

3. A search on jstor.org turns up exactly one published paper focusing on Virginia's children's books, Susan Elizabeth Howe, "The Danish Genesis of Virginia Sorensen's 'Lotte's Locket,'" *Dialogue: A Journal of Mormon Thought* 35, no. 1 (Spring 2002), 113–129. Howe wrote another paper, "Virginia Sorensen for Children," for the Colloquium for Virginia Sorensen, BYU, October 13, 1988, Virginia Sorensen Papers, MSS 1686, box 8, fd. 1, but it never seems to have been published.

4. Oliver LaFarge to Virginia Sorensen, Virginia Sorensen Papers, MSS 1686, box 1, fd. 9.

However, the novels that sprang from Virginia's sojourns were not stories about these various cultures and their people. Rather, they were stories about what happens when that particular culture and people come into contact with another culture and people—novels of cultural confluence. Her first children's novel, *Curious Missie*, started this theme in a small way, simply bringing oral culture into contact with print culture. It takes place in a small farming community in Alabama living on the cusp of change. Their traditional farming methods are being challenged by government agents passing out pamphlets that promote more modern techniques, and Missie's father is resistant: "Missie, some people think they can't even plant cotton without books. But we do not need them." Missie's relentless appetite for answers and reason attracts the county librarian who harnesses Missie's enthusiasm to help bring a bookmobile into the area.

Virginia's second children's novel, *The House Next Door*, takes the stakes much higher, as Gerry, a well-to-do sixteen-year-old Virginian girl, visits her aunt in Salt Lake City. Her aunt is a Presbyterian missionary who helps run a house for "Escaped and Repentant Polygamous Wives," as well as an anti-polygamy newspaper. She instructs Gerry to stay away from the next-door neighbors—a three-wife Mormon family—but to no avail. Similarly, *Around the Corner* follows a ten-year-old Junie, as he disobeys his mother's orders and sneaks around to the other side of the block to meet a family of displaced Appalachians who have taken up temporary residence in a condemned house. Probably the most poignant of these cultural encounters is in *Plain Girl*, where Esther, an Amish girl, is forced to attend a local public school where her interactions with a kind classmate and the sudden appearance of a brother who had abandoned the community throw her into religious turmoil.

In each of Virginia's stories, the protagonist is an ordinary child. None is chosen by destiny, none has a special mission, none is smarter or stronger than average, and none has huge obstacles to overcome. The unique thing about them is their situation. They happen to occupy what Virginia called "the middle,"[5] where two cultures meet. But instead of doing something extraordinary, they do what any

---

5. Virginia Sorensen, "Is It True?—The Novelist and His Materials, *Western Humanities Review* 7, no. 4 (Autumn 1953): 285.

child would do: Gerry looks over the fence at the family next door; Junie sneaks over to listen as the family around the corner plays music on their front porch; Esther reads a note dropped onto her desk by the girl sitting in front of her; Marly wanders over to see where the sweet smell of maple is coming from; Missie asks her teacher where she can find more books.

Ordinary actions. Indeed, one child wrote to Virginia, "What I like about your books ... is that they are about ordinary people doing ordinary things."[6] It seems a banal observation, perhaps even a veiled insult—who would want to read a book about "ordinary people doing ordinary things"? But, in fact, this observation leads us straight to the heart of Virginia's children's novels, where she does something very unique. While most children's novelists express an adult's world view through their stories, Virginia gives full expression to the child's.

Psychologist Alison Gopnik coined the terms "lantern consciousness" and "spotlight consciousness" to delineate the difference between the way children and adults encounter the world. Like a lantern, children's "attention is more widely diffused, allowing the child to take in information from virtually anywhere in her field of awareness, which is quite wide, wider than that of most adults." Virginia described this as a "state of unreasonable wonder."[7] It was a state she herself inhabited as a child. As she wrote when she was thirteen years old, "I love dull days because my thoughts make them colorful and vivid."[8] Adults, on the other hand, have a spotlight consciousness, which gives them "the ability to narrowly focus attention on a goal."[9] Children are explorers and gatherers, adults are producers and meaning makers.

This lantern consciousness is always apparent in Virginia's children's novels, great percentages of which are dedicated to rapt, detailed,

---

6. Virginia Sorensen to Elle Lewis Buell, Virginia Sorensen Papers, MSS 1686, box 4, fd. 5.

7. Sorensen, "Childhood Is a Strange Book."

8. Virginia Sorensen, Diary No. I., Aug. 24, 1925, Virginia Sorensen Papers, MSS 1686, box 9, fd. 2.

9. Michael Pollan, *How to Change Your Mind: What the New Science of Psychedelics Teaches Us About Consciousness, Dying, Addition, Depression, and Transcendence* (New York: Penguin Books, 2018), 325. Pollan draws on Alison Gopnik's book *The Philosophical Baby: What Children's Minds Tell Us About Truth, Love, and the Meaning of Life* (New York: Farrar, Straus and Giroux, 2009).

multi-sensory descriptions of a character's environment, especially if it is a natural environment. As Virginia wrote, "there is plenty of excitement between the door and the gatepost to fill a thousand books."[10] Thus, readers follow her child protagonists as they non-judgmentally bring everything they encounter into their newly forming world view.

Of course, this is exactly what the adults in their lives are afraid of. Gerry's aunt does not want Gerry "contaminated" by the Mormons. Esther's Amish father does not want her to be drawn away from the community the way her brother was. Junie's mother does not want him undercutting their already tenuous position as a Black family working toward middle class.

But the child remains a child, going back and forth between the two worlds and soaking up both, beginning to perceive the strengths and weaknesses of each. Gerry notes that the Mormon family next door, though hardworking, honest, and kind, harbors unexamined prejudices against non-Mormons. Among her non-Mormon relatives and friends, she notes both courage and tunnel vision. Esther is astonished to find that the girl who sits in front of her at school, though she wears a pink dress, is effortlessly kind to her. Meanwhile, Esther's brother, who has been shunned by the community, reminds her that though the Amish ignore outsiders, their dedication to those within the community is unmatched.

Eventually, this middle place does get tense. Esther stews in angst while she rides with her father in their horse-drawn wagon toward school, not knowing how to respond to the kindness of a child she is supposed to ignore, and then again when she goes to church, wondering if she has taken "the first step" away from her community by responding to that kind classmate. Missie and Marly find that their love of the natural world and its creatures is not shared by many of the adults around them, and that the girls are sometimes powerless to save them. Junie finds himself caught between his mother and a local grocery store owner when two of the Appalachian boys he befriends are caught shoplifting. Gerry is eventually locked in her room to keep her away from the Mormons next door.

Admittedly, these times of tension are pretty low-key when we

---

10. Sorensen to Buell.

compare them with the situations in some of the more popular books of the day such as *The Prydain Chronicles*, by Lloyd Alexander, and *The Dark Is Rising* series, by Susan Cooper. In these books, children and young adults are thrust out of their home territory into antagonistic environments where they must struggle against sometimes overwhelming odds to survive. But the survival of Virginia's protagonists is never in question. Marly gets her boots stuck in the mud as a herd of young cattle tramp toward her; Missie scrambles to the top of a boulder to escape a bull whose field she accidentally invades; Junie worries that his antics might cause his mother to go into premature labor; and Esther worries that she'll be caught while retrieving her brother's traditional clothing from a chest in her parents' room. All turn out to be low-stakes, sometimes even comical, situations. That lack of tension permeates Virginia's children's novels. As one Amazon reviewer writes of *Miracles on Maple Hill*, "Nice neighbors, nice descriptions of scenery, nice pace, just nice, nice, nice. Nothing interesting or exciting or intriguing ever happens to the main character."

Why does Virginia take this route? Because she is writing from a child's world view. She once noted that she answers the question, "How can you tell a story for a child, at his level?" by challenging "my interrogator to tell a story to two people—the same story, to an adult and then to a child, and watch himself carefully as he tells it. He will add words and subtract them, he will add explanations and leave them out, he will point to a moral or leave it to point itself out at the climax of the story."[11]

When we compare Virginia's children's books to her novels for adults, we see that the main thing she seems to subtract is conflict. She seems to hide much of the world from her young readers.

Virginia says she had her first lesson in writing for children when her debut, *A Little Lower Than the Angels*, came out. Her two children were amazed by the sight of the book with their mother's name on it and insisted that Virginia read something from it to them for bedtime. She chose a snippet about two children who play with some kittens, but accidentally kill them. "When I had finished, my daughter Beth, then nine years old, sat up in bed with streaming eyes. 'You

---

11. Sorensen, "Childhood Is a Strange Book."

made that story up!' she cried accusingly. 'Why did you have to make the kittens die?' ... I feel sure it is because of her tears ... that I have Marly face death something short of the reality in *Miracles*, and that this seemed right for the story."[12]

Are Virginia's children's novels a kind of "Virginia lite"? Stories that pull emotional punches in deference to the tender feelings of her young audience, eventually rendering her narratives, well, ... boring?

A deeper look shows that rather than trying to hide the "real world" from her young readers, Virginia is instead revealing the importance of childhood's lantern consciousness.

This is different from what a great deal of popular children's literature was doing then (and now). In most children's stories, the child's world is invaded by the adult world, or the child has to venture into the adult world. In both cases, the children must become more adult-like in order to survive or succeed. The child succeeds only because the child changes, putting the childish world behind them. The purpose of most popular children's literature is to show a child progressing toward adulthood.

Virginia takes an utterly different approach. In her stories, childhood is not a stepping stone that needs to be abandoned by the end of the story; rather, childhood *is* the world—its value completely independent of the adult world.

Virginia's insistence on the primacy of the child's world may be confusing to modern readers. Having read *Harry Potter* and *The Hunger Games*, readers expect a hero's journey where the protagonist's success is measured by how many obstacles they overcome—how much the protagonist has "grown." In other words, most of the children's novels today train readers to measure something's value by its proximity to the adult world view. Virginia rejects that measuring stick, insisting that we finally perceive the value of a child's world view.

The title of Virginia's Newbery Medal book, *Miracles on Maple Hill*, is a direct reference to the intrinsic value of Marly's lantern-consciousness experience in the Pennsylvania countryside. Marly considers each new natural encounter she has as an actual miracle,

---

12. Virginia Sorensen, "Newbery Award Acceptance," *Horn Book Magazine* 33, no. 4 (Aug. 1957): 277. The death "short of reality" Sorensen is speaking of is a heart attack Mr. Chris suffers toward the end of *Miracles on Maple Hill*—a heart attack he survives.

and the bulk of the book consists of descriptions of these miracles. Meanwhile, curious Missie, though a great lover of school, is late to her first day of class when she stops to wonder at a flock of geese that has settled nearby. She explores the family's land and finds birds' nests and other animal homes. While picking berries, she comes upon a poisonous snake, which she considers the most beautiful creature she has ever seen. Junie spends hours immersed in the music of the Appalachians living around the corner. Cathy endlessly explores the sights, sounds, and scents of Morocco. As Virginia wrote in the *Western Humanities Review*, "It is not new sights that are important in writing, but new seeing."[13] That is what her children are constantly doing for the reader—lending them a new set of eyes, which are—ironically— the reader's original eyes.

Virginia often provides an adult character in her children's novels that retains some of their lantern consciousness: Mr. Chris (Marly's neighbor) in *Miracles on Maple Hill*; Gerry's father in *The House Next Door*; Fru. Fugal (Lotte's teacher) in *Lotte's Locket*; Dr. Prescot (a veterinarian) in *Friends of the Road*; and Uncle Ben in *Around the Corner*.

But along with this abundance of rapture comes an equal abundance of tragedy. Instances of death in the natural world affect the hearts of Virginia's characters as deeply as the profusion of life. Not everything in *Miracles on Maple Hill* is "nice." Early in the book, Marly is ecstatic to find a nest of baby mice in her bedroom. But when she tells her parents about them, they insist on tossing the baby mice into their old-fashioned oven's inferno. To Marly, this action is as horrifying as a holocaust. Missie casts caution and family loyalty aside when she rebukes her father for burning his fields and rushes into the flaming landscape to save bird nests from being destroyed. When Marly accidentally reveals to some adults that her brother, Joe, has found the warren of a fox family, the siblings go out at midnight to smoke the fox family out of its hole and block the entrances before the adults can massacre the family the next morning. When Missie's brothers kill the poisonous snake she found, chopping at it with shovels, she reacts as though she is witnessing a murder and dismemberment. Similarly, Cathy recoils when she catches a glimpse

---

13. Virginia Sorensen, "Is It True?," 288.

of a ram twitching out the last of its life as blood runs from a stab wound in its neck during a festival in Morocco. That which is banal to the story's adults can be an atrocity of near cosmic proportions to the children. However, these moments of horror punctuate the story only occasionally, soon giving way again to wonders.

But Virginia's focus on (and skill at producing) these transporting passages of lantern consciousness comes at the expense of her plots, which are often so small, they would not even strain the capacity of a short story.

This is not a reflection on Virginia's storytelling skills; after all, the plots of many of her adult novels are compelling. Rather, it reflects her commitment to portraying lantern consciousness throughout the story: remaining in the child's world view, rather than working toward the adult's. The problem is that the workings of lantern consciousness are basically at odds with anything the Western mind would recognize as a story.

We usually conceive of a story as a series of conflicts leading to a resolution. We tell a story to point to an idea. In other words, at their base, stories are a product of spotlight consciousness: beginning at one point, proceeding in a certain direction, and illuminating something at the end. Western audiences read a story specifically *because* of its spotlight consciousness. We feel annoyed, even betrayed, if it turns out that a story has no "point." We expect that an author had gone through a period of lantern-like consciousness as they gathered the raw material for their story, but that they then used their spotlight consciousness to give the material shape. It is the shape that propels the reader's interest in the material.

Virginia is vigilant about placing her child protagonists' lantern consciousness at the core of her stories (giving them free rein to explore the expanse between the front door and the gatepost—or the house next door, or the field out back, or the family around the corner). But lantern consciousness is completely unequipped to create a narrative. All it can do is gather material—go exploring. Virginia recognized this, so she frequently uses the spotlight consciousness of the adult characters—*their* goals and hopes and prejudices—as the banks that direct the flow of the children's explorations, thus creating the shape of her plots. Marly explores the Pennsylvania countryside because it is the

place where her father is recovering from post-traumatic stress disorder. She learns about maple extraction because Mr. Chris lives nearby.
She throws huge effort into the maple harvest because Mr. Chris is
hospitalized. Missie becomes an advocate for a bookmobile because
the country librarian brings her to a county commission meeting. Esther goes to school because the law requires it, and she grapples with
cognitive dissonance because of the tension between larger American
culture and her Amish community. Junie only emerges from the music
of his neighbors because of pressures from his parents and the law.
Gerry goes to Utah on her father's insistence.

Virginia's young protagonists find themselves in the confluence
of cultures, caught in the crossfire of adults' spotlight consciousness:
between Aunt Harriet and the Mormons next door; between the law
and the Appalachians around the corner; between an oral culture
and a print culture; between Amish traditions and American culture;
between the city and the country.

However, the children solve these conflicts not by weighing pros
and cons, not through debate, not by throwing their lot in with loyalty or diversity, but by simply being a child. As Gopnik said, "Each
generation of children confronts a new environment, and their brains
are particularly good at learning and thriving in that environment.
Think of the children of immigrants, or four-year-olds confronted
with an iPhone. Children don't invent these new tools, they don't
create the new environment, but in every generation they build the
kind of brain that can best thrive in it."[14]

Though the two cultures and the people within them start out
each novel in conflict, by the end, the child has either helped them
find a way to accommodate each other to some degree or has found
their own way to navigate between the two. Gerry is able to save
the life of her next-door neighbor's grandfather *because* she knows
the non-Mormon doctor in town—the only doctor not celebrat-
ing Mormon Pioneer Day up the canyon. Then she helps her Aunt
Harriet perceive her next-door neighbors' humanness by keeping an
honest diary. When Junie's mother goes into premature labor, the
family around the corner, whose grandmother is a midwife, helps

14. Pollan, *How to Change Your Mind*, 327.

her deliver the baby *because* of Junie's relationship with them. Then he is able to help them find a new place to live because of his connections with local church and legal authorities. Esther is able to help her estranged brother regain access to the Amish community while simultaneously forging a relationship with an outsider. Marly learns from the Chris family to extract maple syrup, and then, when Mr. Chris falls ill at a critical point, brings in her classmates to help with the harvest.

However, two of Virginia's children's novels take almost no advantage of adults' spotlight consciousness to give her protagonists' lantern consciousness a narrative shape: *Lotte's Locket* and *Friends of the Road.*

Friends of the Road follows Cathy (an American "foreign services brat") as she explores Morocco, becomes friends with Pippa (a girl from England), and raises a lamb. There are a few sad incidents, such as Cathy's dog being shot by a policeman and Pippa falling ill, but they are incidents held in the lantern light. Cathy and Pippa go through a period of lantern consciousness with each other, learning about one another's home cultures and letting go of prejudices, but this process takes up only a small part of the narrative. The book climaxes when Cathy and Pippa lose their way in a large city and, frightened, hole up in a café until they get their bearings; but the scene has little to do with anything that happens previously. It is also the only scene with any tension in it, which is probably why the illustrator chose to portray it on the cover.

Lotte's Locket depicts the Danish girl Lotte as she prepares to follow her mother, who has married an American, to the United States. Dreading the day she must leave, Lotte spends most of the novel soaking in every bit of Danish scenery, history, and culture she possibly can.

The narrative shortcomings of lantern consciousness are especially stark in *Lotte's Locket* because the story starts out with loads of possibilities. A room in Lotte's house is a kind of shrine to eight generations of Lottes, all of whom were christened in the same dress and who are gifted with a locket passed down through the generations. Lotte is next in line to carry on this tradition and add her photograph to the wall. But instead of weaving that tradition into Lotte's adventures and interpreting her departure to America as a new chapter of the Lotte legacy, Virginia leaves it all behind, Lotte leaving the locket in the Lotte room. And the narrative does not follow Lotte to America, never giving her a chance, like many of the heroines of Virginia's previous books, to be the character that bridges two cultures.

However, remember that readers are used to valuing the demands of spotlight consciousness in stories: in that light, the novels are indeed long on material and short on shape. But when considered in the light of lantern consciousness, they are luminous—perfect examples of "unreasonable wonder." If readers want to see the glory of Morocco or Denmark through a child's eyes, these are the books for them.

Virginia's main goal with her children's novels was to show her readers the value of lantern consciousness, to see its effect on the world, and to soak in its magic for as long as we can. The world would be lost without this unique childhood attribute, she says. Children are valuable *because* they are children, not because they are proto-adults.

"'How can I *forget* childhood and how it was?'" she asked. "It is always with me, my childhood, vivid and real and meaningfully, and as the years pass I remember it more and more vividly far back, and the things that happened after I grew up are fading faster and faster. Any old one will tell you of the truth of this. Perhaps when I am eighty I shall write as a child again."[15]

Virginia herself seemed greatly possessed of lantern consciousness. It was one of the qualities that made her such a penetrating, empathetic observer. "It could be," Virginia said in her Newbery Award acceptance speech, "that when at last it seems futile to criticize the endless ills that we are heir to, some of us turn to writing for children because the value of life becomes more and more apparent and we must turn to celebration."[16]

---

15. Sorensen, "Childhood Is a Strange Book."
16. Sorensen, "Newbery Award Acceptance," 284.

EPILOGUE

In her foreword to the 1999 reprint of Virginia Sorensen's *The Evening and the Morning*, Linda Sillitoe, an LDS journalist, novelist, and poet, writes about her young daughter Cynthia, who had gotten to know Virginia shortly before her death in 1991. Virginia had even come to Cynthia's sixth-grade class to discuss her youth novels.

Later, when she was twenty years old, Sillitoe writes, "Cynthia plunged through *The Evening and the Morning*, weeping. She cried, she said later, because the writing was so beautiful; because Virginia was so present; because Virginia was gone ... because she had been too young to converse as one adult talks with another."[1]

That is how I feel after reading Virginia's novels. I desperately miss someone I have never even met.

"Someone like Virginia arouses hunger ... to know intensity, to live in beauty,"[2] Sillitoe writes. That same hunger is what led me to spend a few years of my life reading everything I could possibly find by and about Virginia.

Just her and me. Present. Conversing.

I hope this small biography inspires readers to do a quick search at their local library for one of Virginia's novels, find an ebook, or perhaps scour the bargain bins of eBay on the off chance that they, too, might be one of the lucky few who become possessed of this magnificent hunger.

---

1. Linda Sillitoe, foreword to Virginia Sorensen, *The Evening and the Morning* (Salt Lake City: Signature Books, 1999), viii–ix.

2. Sillitoe, foreword, viii.

INDEX